C. Michael Hall
Editor

Wine, Food, and Tourism Marketing

Wine, Food, and Tourism Marketing has been co-published simultaneously as Journal of Travel & Tourism Marketing, Volume 14, Numbers 3/4 2003.

Pre-publication REVIEWS, COMMENTARIES, EVALUATIONS . . .

" A VALUABLE RESOURCE for all who research, practice, or facilitate food and wine tourism. As a lover of travel, good food, and wine, the mark of a memorable holiday, for me, is the coincidence of all three. Despite having a wealth of natural edible assets the equal of our acclaimed cultural and scenic attractions, few visitors rate food as a reason for holidaying in Scotland. Still fewer would recognize us as a gastronomic tourism destination. But all the ingredients are here, only the joining-up initiatives are in short supply. In this book C. Michael Hall has illustrated how similar challenges and opportunities are tackled around the world."

Wendy Barrie, MHCIMA, MREHIS MInstD, DipHEc
Director, www.scottishfoodguide.com

More pre-publication
REVIEWS, COMMENTARIES, EVALUATIONS . . .

"**E**XCELLENT. . . . HIGHLY RECOM-
MENDED. C. Michael Hall takes
us on a new journey to explore the
previously unexplored field of marketing in relation to wine, food, and
tourism. This landmark book brings
the subject to life with a range of
COMPREHENSIVE, INFORMATIVE contributions from a number of countries. The integration of food with
wine and tourism is a first and the
book makes a significant contribution to our thinking on this subject."

Ross K. Dowling, PhD
*Foundation Professor of Tourism
and Head
School of Marketing
Tourism & Leisure
Edith Cowan University, Australia*

THHP

The Haworth Hospitality Press®
An Imprint of The Haworth Press, Inc.

New York • London • Victoria (AU)
www.HaworthPress.com

Wine, Food, and Tourism Marketing

Wine, Food, and Tourism Marketing has been co-published simultaneously as *Journal of Travel & Tourism Marketing,* Volume 14, Numbers 3/4 2003.

The *Journal of Travel & Tourism Marketing*™ Monographic "Separates"

Editor-in-Chief: K. S. (Kaye) Chon

Below is a list of "separates," which in serials librarianship means a special issue simultaneously published as a special journal issue or double-issue *and* as a "separate" hardbound monograph. (This is a format which we also call a "DocuSerial.")

"Separates" are published because specialized libraries or professionals may wish to purchase a specific thematic issue by itself in a format which can be separately cataloged and shelved, as opposed to purchasing the journal on an on-going basis. Faculty members may also more easily consider a "separate" for classroom adoption.

"Separates" are carefully classified separately with the major book jobbers so that the journal tie-in can be noted on new book order slips to avoid duplicate purchasing.

You may wish to visit Haworth's website at . . .

http://www.HaworthPress.com

. . . to search our online catalog for complete tables of contents of these separates and related publications.

You may also call 1-800-HAWORTH (outside US/Canada: 607-722-5857), or Fax 1-800-895-0582 (outside US/Canada: 607-771-0012), or e-mail at:

docdelivery@haworthpress.com

Wine, Food, and Tourism Marketing, edited by C. Michael Hall, PhD, (Vol. 14, No. 3/4, 2003). *"ONE OF THE WORLD'S FOREMOST RESEARCHERS IN CULINARY TOURISM TAKES THE FIELD TO A NEW LEVEL . . ." (Erik Wolf, MA, Director, International Culinary Tourism Association)*

Tourism Forecasting and Marketing, edited by Kevin K. F. Wong, PhD, and Haiyan Song, PhD, (Vol. 13, No. 1/2, 2002). *"A VALUABLE RESOURCE for policymakers in both the private and public sectors . . . Makes a significant contribution to the field of tourism forecasting by bringing together many different research methodologies with data on tourism flows from around the world." (Pauline J. Sheldon, PhD, Interim Dean and Professor, School of Travel Industry Management, University of Hawaii at Manoa)*

Japanese Tourists: Socio-Economic, Marketing and Psychological Analysis, edited by K. S. (Kaye) Chon, Tustomo Inagaki, and Taji Ohashi (Vol. 9, No. 1/2, 2000). *Presents recent studies on the socioeconomic, marketing, and psychological analysis of Japanese tourists.*

Geography and Tourism Marketing, edited by Martin Oppermann, PhD (Vol. 6, No. 3/4, 1997). *"Casts much light on how insights from geography can be applied to, and gained from, tourism promotion. . . . Well-written, informative, and interesting, and the issues are important." (David Harrison, PhD, Co-ordinator of Tourism Studies, School of Social and Economic Development, University of the South Pacific, Suva, Fiji)*

Marketing Issues in Pacific Area Tourism, edited by John C. Crotts, PhD, and Chris A. Ryan, PhD (Vol. 6, No. 1, 1997). *"A significant volume on the marketing issues that face the region. Nicely complements existing texts and will carve its own distinctive niche as a reference work. . . . Valuable to students of tourism marketing both inside and outside of the Pacific region." (C. Michael Hall, PhD, Professor and Chairperson, Tourism and Services Management, Victoria University of Wellington, New Zealand)*

Recent Advances in Tourism Marketing Research, edited by Daniel R. Fesenmaier, PhD, Joseph T. O'Leary, PhD, and Muzaffer Uysal, PhD (Vol. 5, No. 2/3, 1996). *"This book clearly marks the current advancement in tourism marketing research. . . . Tourism marketing researchers and academics can gain useful insights by reading this text." (Journal of the Academy of Marketing Science)*

Economic Psychology of Travel and Tourism, edited by John C. Crotts, PhD, and W. Fred van Raaij, PhD (Vol. 3, No. 3, 1995). *"A fresh and innovative volume that expands our understanding of consumers in the tourism market. . . . Will be a useful reference for scholars and graduate students working in tourism psychology and marketing." (Dr. Stephen L. J. Smith, Professor, Department of Recreation and Leisure Studies, University of Waterloo, Ontario, Canada)*

Communication and Channel Systems in Tourism Marketing, edited by Muzaffer Uysal, PhD, and Daniel R. Fesenmaier, PhD (Vol. 2, No. 2/3, 1994). *"Loaded with information on a variety of topics that provides readers with a solid background of the topic as well as introduces them to new ideas. . . . A valuable resource." (Robert M. O'Halloran, PhD, Associate Professor, School of Hotel, Restaurant & Tourism, University of Denver)*

Published by

The Haworth Hospitality Press®, 10 Alice Street, Binghamton, NY 13904-1580 USA

The Haworth Hospitality Press® is an imprint of The Haworth Press, Inc., 10 Alice Street, Binghamton, NY 13904-1580 USA.

Wine, Food, and Tourism Marketing has been co-published simultaneously as *Journal of Travel & Tourism Marketing,* Volume 14, Numbers 3/4 2003.

The development, preparation, and publication of this work has been undertaken with great care. However, the publisher, employees, editors, and agents of The Haworth Press and all imprints of The Haworth Press, Inc., including The Haworth Medical Press® and The Pharmaceutical Products Press®, are not responsible for any errors contained herein or for consequences that may ensue from use of materials or information contained in this work. Opinions expressed by the author(s) are not necessarily those of The Haworth Press, Inc.

Cover design by Brooke R. Stiles

Library of Congress Cataloging-in-Publication Data

Wine, food, and tourism marketing / C. Michael Hall, editor.
       p. cm.
Includes bibliographical references and index.
       ISBN 0-7890-0082-2 (hard cover : alk. paper) – ISBN 0-7890-0106-3 (soft cover : alk. paper)
1. Wine and wine making. 2. Tourism–Marketing. I. Hall, Colin Michael, 1961-
TP548.5.T68W56 2004
338.4'791–dc22
                                                                                        2003017504

Wine, Food, and Tourism Marketing

C. Michael Hall
Editor

Wine, Food, and Tourism Marketing has been co-published simultaneously as *Journal of Travel & Tourism Marketing*, Volume 14, Numbers 3/4 2003.

The Haworth Hospitality Press®
An Imprint of The Haworth Press, Inc.

New York • London • Victoria (AU)
www.HaworthPress.com

Indexing, Abstracting & Website/Internet Coverage

This section provides you with a list of major indexing & abstracting services. That is to say, each service began covering this periodical during the year noted in the right column. Most Websites which are listed below have indicated that they will either post, disseminate, compile, archive, cite or alert their own Website users with research-based content from this work. (This list is as current as the copyright date of this publication.)

(continued)

* Exact start date to come.

Special Bibliographic Notes related to special journal issues (separates) and indexing/abstracting:

- indexing/abstracting services in this list will also cover material in any "separate" that is co-published simultaneously with Haworth's special thematic journal issue or DocuSerial. Indexing/abstracting usually covers material at the article/chapter level.
- monographic co-editions are intended for either non-subscribers or libraries which intend to purchase a second copy for their circulating collections.
- monographic co-editions are reported to all jobbers/wholesalers/approval plans. The source journal is listed as the "series" to assist the prevention of duplicate purchasing in the same manner utilized for books-in-series.
- to facilitate user/access services all indexing/abstracting services are encouraged to utilize the co-indexing entry note indicated at the bottom of the first page of each article/chapter/contribution.
- this is intended to assist a library user of any reference tool (whether print, electronic, online, or CD-ROM) to locate the monographic version if the library has purchased this version but not a subscription to the source journal.
- individual articles/chapters in any Haworth publication are also available through the Haworth Document Delivery Service (HDDS).

Wine, Food, and Tourism Marketing

CONTENTS

ABOUT THE EDITOR

C. Michael Hall, PhD, is Head of the Department of Tourism at the University of Otago in New Zealand. He is Honorary Professor of the Department of Marketing, University of Stirling in Scotland and Honorary Visiting Professor in the School of Leisure and Food Management at Sheffield Hallam University in England. He is Chairperson of the International Geographical Union Commission on Tourism, Leisure, and Global Change and in 1995 was elected as a member of the International Academy for the Study of Tourism.

Preface

Food and wine mean more than just eating and drinking. Food relates to issues of identity, culture, production, consumption, and increasingly, given the debate that surrounds the genetic engineering, food labelling and agricultural production subsidies, issues of sustainability. Food is also a major component of the tourism product. Whether in the background of the tourism experience as the meal advertised in the resort brochure or the meal at the local restaurant, or in the foreground as in the case of special interest cuisine or wine tourism, and the role of certain foods, cooking schools, restaurants and chefs as visitor attractions in their own right, food is a significant part of tourism. For many years the common understanding of the food-tourism relationship in the field of tourism studies was through the provision of food for tourists in restaurants, resorts or hotels. However, more recently food has come to be recognised as part of the local culture which tourists consume, as an element of regional tourism promotion, a potential component of local agricultural and economic development, as a differentiated product in a competitive destination market, as an indicator of globalisation, and as something which is in itself affected by the consumption patterns and perceived preferences of tourists (Hall et al., 2003). Food, for so long in the background of tourism research, has therefore become a focus of increased scrutiny by academics and researchers not only in understanding the manner in which tourism is part of wider economic, socio-cultural, and environmental systems but also how it may contrib-

C. Michael Hall is Professor and Head of Department, Department of Tourism, School of Business, University of Otago, Dunedin, New Zealand (E-mail: cmhall@business.otago.ac.nz).

[Haworth co-indexing entry note]: "Preface." Hall, C. Michael. Co-published simultaneously in *Journal of Travel & Tourism Marketing* (The Haworth Hospitality Press, an imprint of The Haworth Press, Inc.) Vol. 14, No. 3/4, 2003, pp. xiii-xiv; and: *Wine, Food, and Tourism Marketing* (ed: C. Michael Hall) The Haworth Hospitality Press, an imprint of The Haworth Press, Inc., 2003, pp. xiii-xiv. Single or multiple copies of this article are available for a fee from The Haworth Document Delivery Service [1-800-HAWORTH, 9:00 a.m. - 5:00 p.m. (EST). E-mail address: docdelivery@haworthpress. com].

http://www.haworthpress.com/store/product.asp?sku=J073
xiii

ute to tourism marketing strategies at the level of both the destination and the firm.

The various contributions to this volume highlight a wide variety of issues associated with food and wine marketing in different countries and at different scales. These include the role of government in promoting food and wine tourism (Westering's and Niel) and the broader development of marketing policies (Boyne et al.); the role of food and wine in destination marketing (du Rand et al.) and positioning (Frochot; Hashimoto and Telfer); food and wine and product development at both regional and firm levels (Sharples; Demhardt); wine market segmentation (Williams and Dossa); and the relationship between wine tourism and seasonality (Mitchell and Hall). The various contributions are representative of some of the major concerns in food and wine marketing and it is hoped that they further contribute not only to increased academic interest in wine and food tourism marketing but also to the practical contribution that such research can make to destination development and inter-sectoral cooperation.

C. Michael Hall

REFERENCE

Hall, C.M., Sharples, E., Mitchell, R., Cambourne, B., & Macionis, N. (Eds.) (2003) *Food Tourism Around the World: Development, Management and Markets.* Oxford: Butterworth-Heinemann.

Non-Resident Wine Tourist Markets: Implications for British Columbia's Emerging Wine Tourism Industry

Peter W. Williams
Karim B. Dossa

SUMMARY. This paper describes key travel traits of non-resident visitors to British Columbia's wine tourism destinations. It identifies Generalist and Immersionist as being important segments of this market that merit particular attention in future destination management planning and marketing initiatives. It uses an importance-performance analysis framework to determine the key areas for management activity that need to be addressed in order to meet the travel product needs of each of these segments. The paper concludes by recommending a range of strategic initiatives that should be used by the wine industry and its tourism partners to elevate the appeal of BC wine destinations in the international marketplace. While specific to the

Peter W. Williams is Professor, School of Resource Management, and Director, Centre for Tourism Policy and Research, Simon Fraser University. Karim B. Dossa is Senior Research Associate, Centre for Tourism Policy and Research, Simon Fraser University.

Address correspondence to: Peter W. Williams, Director, Centre for Tourism Policy and Research, Simon Fraser University, Burnaby, BC V5A 1S6, Canada (E-mail: peter_williams@sfu.ca).

[Haworth co-indexing entry note]: "Non-Resident Wine Tourist Markets: Implications for British Columbia's Emerging Wine Tourism Industry." Williams, Peter W., and Karim B. Dossa. Co-published simultaneously in *Journal of Travel & Tourism Marketing* (The Haworth Hospitality Press, an imprint of The Haworth Press, Inc.) Vol. 14, No. 3/4, 2003, pp. 1-34; and: *Wine, Food, and Tourism Marketing* (ed: C. Michael Hall) The Haworth Hospitality Press, an imprint of The Haworth Press, Inc., 2003, pp. 1-34. Single or multiple copies of this article are available for a fee from The Haworth Document Delivery Service [1-800-HAWORTH, 9:00 a.m. - 5:00 p.m. (EST). E-mail address: docdelivery@haworthpress.com].

http://www.haworthpress.com/store/product.asp?sku=J073
10.1300/J073v14n03_01

1

BC case, these recommendations may have applicability in a wider range of wine tourism settings. *[Article copies available for a fee from The Haworth Document Delivery Service: 1-800-HAWORTH. E-mail address: <docdelivery@haworthpress. com> Website: <http://www.HaworthPress.com> © 2003 by The Haworth Press, Inc. All rights reserved.]*

KEYWORDS. Non-resident wine tourists, British Columbia, market segments

INTRODUCTION

"Wine making is quite a simple business, only the first 200 years are difficult," Baroness Philippine de Rothshcild likes to tell visitors to her chateau near Bordeaux (Rachman, 1999). Since the mid-1970s a spate of new wines and wineries have emerged around the globe making it readily apparent that a long history of wine making is not needed to produce competitive wine products. Much to the chagrin of many Old World wine producers, Californian wine makers have become part of the global wine establishment. They in turn are disquieted by the success of upstart producers in Washington and Oregon, Australia, Chile, New Zealand, Argentina, South Africa, Eastern Europe and Canada. Given the significant and growing glut of wine products in most of these locations, it is not surprising that many of these regions are shifting some of their focus into the development of wine tourism operations. In varying instances, the move to wine tourism is driven by desires to use wine tourism as a tool for facilitating new product testing; building brand loyalty; increasing profit margins; developing consumer marketing intelligence; providing additional sales outlets; and heightening consumer awareness and understanding of wine products (Dodd, 1995).

The importance of this movement to wine tourism operations is expressed in several contexts. For example, growing domestic and international competition has forced many Canadian wine producers to refocus portions of their marketing resources toward encouraging visitors to make their wine purchases at on-site winery retail outlets (Saunders, 1996). Similarly, the vast majority of American wineries rely primarily on tourism generated wine revenues for their survival. This situation has been driven by prohibitive cost constraints associated with marketing their wine products beyond local regions and the fact that profit margins are highest at the cellar door. For instance, many wineries in New York and Washington State rely almost exclusively on direct sales to visitors (Folwell & Grassell, 1989). Other illustrations of the importance of such wine tourism initiatives include: wineries in the Margaret River wine region of Australia reporting that cellar door wine sales accounted for an average of 34% of total revenues (King & Morris, 1997); Clare and Barossa Valleys wineries in Southern Australia indicating that between 20% and 30% of total sales annually were associated with on-site wine purchases (Reilly, 1996); and wineries in France estimating that direct sales comprised about 19% of Burgundy's and 23% of Alsace's wine revenues (Choisy, 1996). In all of these cases, the wineries depended on a combination of resident (domestic) and non-resident (international) visitors for these purchases.

From a management perspective, information concerning resident wine consumers and to a lesser extent local wine tourists is becoming more abundant. Collected primarily for strategic product development and marketing purposes, it typically describes consumer demographics, purchasing behavior, decision-making processes, and some linkages with other activities in wine regions (e.g., Dodd & Bigotte, 1995; Maddern & Golledge, 1996; Beverland et al., 1998, Longo, 1999; Mitchell et al., 1999; Hall et al., 2000). While these findings suggest the existence of several commonalties in the traits of winery visitors, there is a growing realization that distinct geographic, socio-demographic and behavioral sub-segments of the wine tourist market exist (O'Neill & Charters, 1999; Hall et al., 2000; Machin, 2000; Mitchell & Hall, 2001).

Geographic sub-segments of this market become especially important to understand, as many emerging wine tourism destinations are beginning to focus their advertising resources on attracting travellers from international regions. This is particularly the case in jurisdictions such as British Columbia, where resources for international marketing are primarily dedicated to country-specific promotion programs (TBC, 2001). However, without empirical information concerning the characteristics of these non-local markets, what constitutes a "wine country experience" for destination management organizations and other marketers tends to be primarily intuitive in character (Getz, 1999; Williams, 2001).

The limited number of existing empirical studies that have examined non-local travel markets suggest that many opportunities to strengthen the non-resident or international component of wine tourism markets exist. For instance, in Australia, an international visitor survey indicated that approximately 10% of the total visitors to Australia in 1996 visited wineries. Those countries which generated the most winery visitors were the United Kingdom (25% of all UK visitors), Canada (24%), and Germany (18%). Wine visitors tended to be middle aged (40-49 years) people evenly distributed between men and women (Robins 1999). In Southern Australia, this propensity to visit wineries was even more pronounced. About 40% of all international visitors to that region included a visit to a winery in their travel agendas. This translated into about 100,000 cellar door visitors in 1997 (SATC, 1997).

Similarly, interest in wine tourism was also high on the preference lists of a sizeable proportion of international visitors to New Zealand. About 18% of overseas visitors to New Zealand had visited a winery (Lawson et al., 1997). These results compare with those of the New Zealand International Visitors Survey (1995-96) which found 13% of international visitors had either gone on a wine trail or visited a vineyard during their stay (NZTB, 1997). An earlier study by the same organization discovered that about 12% of international visitors had participated in wine tasting (NZTB, 1993).

Beyond these estimations of existing market penetration levels, little is known about the socio-demographic, travel product preferences and behaviors of non-resident wine tourism travel markets. In this regard, Johnson (1998) suggests that information concerning the motivations of such travellers (in addition to other "pull" factors) can help to usefully identify useful market niches. Such information is especially important in helping tourism operators respond with products and services suited to the subtleties of market demand.

Because of the expanding competition for wine consumers and tourists in many grape growing regions around the globe, and especially in North America, there is a growing need for non-resident wine tourist market information that can be used for product development and marketing activities. It is in this context that the following research is conducted. Its purpose is to contribute to academic and industry understanding of the dominant and differentiating characteristics of non-resident wine tourists as reported by travelers themselves. It focuses on examining the traits (especially those motivational characteristics) of non-resident visitors to British Columbia's emerging wine producing regions.

BRITISH COLUMBIA WINE PRODUCING DESTINATIONS

In the 1860s, British Columbia's first grapevines were planted in the scenic and climatically moderate Okanagan Valley. Located about 400 km from Vancouver in the Canadian Rockies, commercial grape growing began there in the 1920s, followed by commercial wine making in the 1930s. In the early stages of production, the industry produced dessert and fortified wines using Lambrusca grapes. By the 1960s, it had moved to producing "pop" and "sparkling" wines from hybrid grapes. During the mid- to late 1980s significant changes to the region's wine industry occurred. These changes were in response to the advent of North American and broader free trade agreements, as well as growing consumer and industry demand for improved product quality credibility. Probably the most significant change involved the grape growing industry, with government support, aggressively removing lower quality grape producing vines and replacing them with higher quality vinifera. The result of these actions has been dramatic.

In a few short years, there has been a rapid expansion in BC agricultural lands dedicated to quality grape production. The grape producing area has increased by 182%, from 1,480 in 1990 to 4,184 in 1999 (average annual increase of 12.3%). Furthermore, it is predicted that land allocated to grape producing will expand to 5,684 acres by 2003. This represents more than double the total producing acreage that existed as recently as 1997 (BCWI, 1998/1999).

These lands have become very productive. In 1999, a total of 11,284 (short) tons of wine grapes were produced in BC. This represented an increase of 134% over 1990's total of 4,827 tons. As well, future increases in wine production are expected to bring BC's total wine grape production to about 21,687 tons by 2004, almost double the amount produced in 1999. In keeping with increases in grape quality, the average price per ton for BC wine grapes has increased by 45.2% since 1990 (average annual increase of 4.2%), and wines produced from these grape have followed suit (46.9% overall increase between 1995 and 1999). Furthermore between 1990 to 1999, the number of wineries in BC almost tripled from 21 to 61, with most of the growth occurring in the small farm-based, family-operated wineries category (BCWI, 1999).

Despite these positive indicators, the BC wine industry has been confronted with some significant challenges to its long-term economic sustainability. Not the least of these challenges is related to wine sales, which have not kept pace with the region's production capacity. Wine sales in BC have increased only slightly over the last five years, with total litre sales increasing only 3.4% between the approximately 33.4 million litres sold in 1995 and the 34.6 million litres sold in 1999 (BCWI, 1999). This flat performance has been attributed to a relatively weak provincial economy; higher BC product price points; non-aggressive wine distribution channels; external competition from other wine producing regions; and generally low awareness of the internationally competitive quality of BC wines. In response, the wine industry of BC has commenced initiatives to market its product domestically and internationally via alternative distribution channels such as wine tourism. Over 70% of existing BC wineries are now engaged in activities promoting wine tourism opportunities at their sites. However, like so many other emerging wine tourism destinations, to do this effectively, they require more specific information concerning the market characteristics and tourism product preferences of its non-resident markets. This paper reports on several of these characteristics for non-resident wine tourists visiting BC.

METHOD

To provide insights into the defining characteristics of the non-resident wine tourism market in British Columbia a three-phase investigation was conducted. Primary data for the research was derived from the BC Visitor Study (TBC, 1997). In this study, non-resident visitors were those travellers who did not reside in the province of British Columbia but visited the province during the survey period. They were randomly intercepted at 40 entry sites into the province over a one-year period between April 1995 and March 1996. They were asked to record their responses to a range of travel related questions on a Leisure Travel survey instrument and then mail back the completed questionnaire. The questions asked were related to the socio-demographic, travel and trip motivation characteristics, as well as their trip planning, activity, product preferences, and expenditures of these non-resident travelers to BC.

This paper analyses responses of 261 of the 2,694 respondents who completed this survey, and who indicated that they had included a visit to a winery/farm during their BC travels within the study period. Because of the very limited number of farm-based vacation opportunities in the province, and the growing promotion of BC wineries as tourism attractions, it was assumed that the vast majority of these respondents were wine tourists.

The responses provided by these "wine" tourists provided the basis for the three-phased analysis presented in this paper. The first phase described and compared the character of this cohort of travelers with those of all other non-resident travelers to the province. The overriding hypothesis examined in this phase of the research was that non-resident wine tourists exhibited travel attitudes and behaviors which clearly distinguished them from other non-resident visitors to the province. Chi-square and t-tests were used where appropriate to test for significant differences in the responses of these two cohorts of travelers.

In the second phase of this research, a more focussed probe was conducted to identify distinct sub-segments of BC's wine tourist market (Johnson, 1998; MTV, 1995). The overriding research question was "do distinct subsets of non-resident wine tourist markets exist which exhibit significant differences in their socio-demographic, motivational, and behavioral characteristics?" Initially this second research phase used a "motivation or benefit based" hierarchical cluster analysis using Wards method and Squared Euclidean distances to identify wine tourist market clusters, which were distinctive in terms of the levels of importance they placed on a range of travel motivators (SPSS, 1997). There was some sample attrition due to the dropping of cases with missing information on one or more of the clustering variables. Two wine tourist clusters were generated and subsequently analyzed using chi-square and t-tests (where appropriate) to establish the extent to which these market niches differed with respect to their socio-demographic, attitudinal and behavioral traits. Only differences statistically significant at the .05 level of probability or greater are reported in this paper.

In the third and final phase of this research, an importance-performance analysis (IPA) was undertaken to help identify those areas for strategic product development and marketing (Martilla & James, 1977). IPAs have been applied in a number of strategic product development and marketing settings with relatively little modification for more than two decades (Parasuraman et al., 1994). In a tourism and recreation management context, they have been used to help assess product and service quality associated with attractions and destinations such as visitor bureaus (Chon et al., 1988), ski resorts (Hudson & Shephard, 1998), parks settings (Crompton et al., 1991), and recreation centers (Howat et al., 1996).

In this study's IPA, several tourism destination attributes were rated by the non-resident wine tourists with respect to how important each factor was in their decision to visit BC. The respondents also indicated how satisfied they were with each of these attributes after their trip to BC had been completed. Based on the responses received, the IPA involved two phases. In the initial phase, the gap in mean scores between stated importance and performance was measured (Crompton & MacKay, 1988). This provided a basis for identifying the relative levels of disconfirmation associated with each of the destination attributes (Parasuraman et al., 1994). The second phase of the IPA involved the development of two-dimensional matrices which graphically compared the mean attribute performance and importance scores obtained from the respondents (Slack, 1994). These matrices were used to identify high priority attributes for improvement and to provide guidance for strategy formulation (Hansen & Bush, 1999). While the scaling of the IPA matrix axes was based on 5-point importance-performance response scales, the quadrant boundaries for determining strategies were somewhat arbitrary–the focus being on the relative positioning of the various importance-performance points in the matrix. Overall, strategy development resulting from the interpretation of the resulting matrix graphs focussed on shifting resources and efforts from providing attributes of low importance and high performance to those of high importance but low performance (Sampson & Showalter, 1999). So as to avoid the potential for unnecessary visitor displacement from the destination (Kuss et al., 1990; Vaske et al., 1996), the IPAs were conducted on the sub-segments of the BC non-resident wine tourist markets identified in the second phase of the study.

OVERALL FINDINGS

Market Penetration

About 9.7% of all non-resident visitors surveyed had visited a farm or farm/winery on their trip. This level of market penetration by non-resident travellers was lower than that associated with other wine producing regions reviewed.

Socio-Demographic Characteristics

Non-resident wine tourists tended to be relatively well educated, employed, male, late baby boomers. Compared to other non-resident visitors, they tended to be younger, better educated, and less well paid (Table 1).

Travel Philosophies

Overall, non-resident wine tourists strongly supported using money for travel purposes, but within planned and value conscious guidelines. However, their other travel philosophies were significantly different from non-resident travellers in several ways. In particular, they tended

TABLE 1. Most Frequent Socio-Demographic Characteristics of Non-Resident Wine Tourists

Characteristic	Visited Wineries	Did Not Visit Wineries
Education	Some college/university (30.0%)	College/university degree (25.8%)
Employment Status	Employed full time (41.7%)	Employed full time (40.7%)
Gender	Male (54.1%)	Female (54.1%)
Total Annual Household Income	$20,000 to under $40,000 (31.2%)	$60,000 to under $80,000 (22.9%)
Average Age	42.9	47.3

to be significantly less impulsive and adventurous in their travel habits, preferring to select destinations with which they were more familiar, planning their trips in advance, taking part in guided tours and packaged trips, seeking less expensive and shorter trips (Table 2).

Destination Selection Factors

For non-resident wine tourists, the most important reasons for selecting BC as a destination were related to the region's natural and social attributes. They placed particular importance on selecting destinations which afforded them opportunities to experience scenic and mountainous areas, meet friendly and hospitable people, visit family oriented places, as well as see and do a wide range of things.

As a group, non-resident wine tourists were significantly more motivated than their non-wine tourist counterparts to visit places which kept them active and engaged both physically and socially. For instance, when choosing BC as a destination, non-resident wine tourists were significantly more apt to place importance on opportunities to: attend sporting events, view wildlife and birds, enjoy nightlife, have a variety of things to see and do, visit friends and relatives, visit clean cities and towns, as well as experience museums and art galleries (Table 3).

Trip Characteristics

Non-resident wine tourists took an average of more that 6 leisure trips outside their home region in the three years preceding the BC Visi-

TABLE 2. Differentiating Non-Resident Wine Tourist Travel Philosophies

	Mean Response *			
Travel Philosophies	Visited Wineries	Did Not Visit Wineries	t	Sig.
I usually choose vacation places where I have been before	2.65	2.23	9.538	0.000
I often choose vacation places that I have heard about from friends who have been there before	3.14	2.89	5.955	0.000
I do not really like to travel	1.54	1.33	5.328	0.000
I like to have all my travel arrangements made before I start out on my trip	3.19	2.98	4.802	0.000
I prefer to go on guided tours when vacationing	2.02	1.82	4.180	0.000
In any one year I would rather take a number of short vacations instead of one long vacation	2.99	2.82	3.536	0.000
I often look for special travel discounts	3.08	2.93	3.144	0.002
I think it is worth paying more to get luxuries and extras on a trip	2.41	2.53	-2.523	0.012

*Mean responses are sorted in descending order (by absolute magnitude of the t value) based on a scale ranging from 1 = strongly disagree to 4 = strongly agree. In other words, the higher the mean, the higher is the level of agreement.

tor study. About a third of these trips were to British Columbia. While they traveled less frequently and went to BC less often than their non-wine tourist counterparts, they tended to travel in larger groups and stay longer in the destination when they did visit. They also spent significantly more while on their trips (Table 4).

Activity Patterns

While traveling in the province, the vast majority of them participated in sightseeing (95%), shopping (93%), dining out (90%), casual walking (89%) and visiting natural displays and gardens (84%). As a group they were much more active than their non-wine tourism counterparts. In almost all activities investigated, significantly larger proportions of them took part in these pursuits. They were especially more active than other travelers with respect to pursuing a range of water based, mechanized and sporting activities (Table 5).

General Trip Element Satisfaction Levels

While the overall levels of satisfaction with their trip to BC tended to be relatively high, non-resident wine tourists tended to be less satisfied than were other visitors to the province. These differences in satisfaction with general trip elements were most evident with respect to the ease of getting to BC, the overall quality of city activities, restaurants,

TABLE 3. Differentiating Non-Resident Destination Selection Factors

Destination Selection Factors	Mean Response*		t	Sig.
	Visited Wineries	Did Not Visit		
Attending sporting events	2.04	1.52	11.255	0.000
Experiencing and seeing a mountain area	3.49	3.00	8.574	0.000
Enjoying night life and entertainment	2.21	1.77	8.424	0.000
Having a variety of things to see and do	3.44	3.04	7.231	0.000
Viewing wildlife and birds	3.07	2.66	6.941	0.000
Visiting clean cities and towns	3.49	3.12	6.904	0.000
Going to a place that is good for the family	3.26	2.80	6.688	0.000
Visiting a place where people speak my language	3.09	2.70	6.428	0.000
Participating in outdoor activities	3.00	2.60	6.224	0.000
Visiting attractions such as museums, art galleries, zoos, etc.	2.75	2.39	6.050	0.000
Going to place I've heard about from friends or relatives	2.93	2.57	5.789	0.000
Visiting cities and/or towns	2.96	2.65	5.548	0.000
Experiencing and seeing a coastal area	2.98	2.62	5.451	0.000
Doing daring and adventuresome activities	2.04	1.75	5.277	0.000
Being physically active	3.04	2.73	5.230	0.000
Visiting places with unique and interesting restaurants	2.85	2.57	5.024	0.000
Visiting scenic areas	3.67	3.44	5.016	0.000
Travelling to places where I feel safe and secure	3.52	3.27	4.667	0.000
Highway transportation within BC	3.06	2.79	4.585	0.000
Getting a good currency exchange rate	2.87	2.56	4.571	0.000
Learning about Native (Indian) culture and art	2.16	1.91	4.521	0.000
Visiting friends and relatives	2.89	2.57	3.999	0.000
Going to places with friendly and hospitable people	3.45	3.24	3.661	0.000
Visiting wilderness and undisturbed areas	2.46	2.24	3.434	0.001
Having the opportunity to shop	2.71	2.53	3.208	0.001
Visiting a place that takes good care of its environment	3.37	3.20	3.162	0.002
Learning new things, increasing my knowledge	3.10	2.93	3.018	0.003
Indulging in luxury such as staying in first class hotels	2.02	1.85	3.009	0.003
Getting value for the cost of the trip	3.34	3.19	2.945	0.003
Getting to know local people	2.55	2.39	2.907	0.004

*Mean responses are sorted in descending order (by absolute magnitude of the t value) based on a scale ranging from 1 = not at all important to 4 = very important.

accommodation and attractions/culture/events as well as getting value for their money (Table 6).

Activity Satisfaction Levels

Similarly, their satisfaction levels with those pursuits that they took part in were significantly less than those expressed by their non-wine

TABLE 4. Differentiating Non-Resident Trip Characteristics

Trip Characteristics	Mean Response		t	Sig.
	Visited Wineries	Did Not Visit Wineries		
Trips taken for leisure outside of home state/province in the past three years	6.08	7.44	-2.814	0.005
Trips to B.C.	2.66	3.62	-2.675	0.008
Travel party size	2.76	2.43	3.090	0.002
Length of stay in BC	10.54	7.55	7.626	0.000
Total household trip expenditures expenses within BC (in dollars) *	1,259.61	970.44	3.628	0.000

*All expenditures are in Canadian dollars and include taxes.

tourism counterparts. This lower level of satisfaction was expressed with respect to a wide range of active, passive, natural and cultural endeavors (Table 7).

Service and Facility Satisfaction Levels

When compared to their non-wine tourist counterparts, non-resident wine tourists were also significantly more dissatisfied with the performance of those destination selection factors that had originally brought them to BC. Wine tourists expressed significantly more dissatisfaction especially with respect to their ability to: experience luxury accommodation, adventuresome activity, visit places good for the family, meet friendly and hospitable people, and be physically active (Table 8).

WINE TOURIST MARKET NICHES

The cluster analysis conducted in this research helped to identify two distinct non-resident wine tourism market niches. They were labeled as being either Generalist or Immersionist market segments.

Generalists

Generalists comprised about 60% of the non-resident wine tourism market. This group was motivated to travel by opportunities to visit a

TABLE 5. Differentiating Non-Resident Trip Activities

Activities Pursued	Percentage of Respondents		X^2	Sig.
	Visited Wineries	Did Not Visit Wineries		
Lake house boating	36.0	1.0	1,110.4879	0.000
Horseback riding	37.3	2.8	783.80242	0.000
Lake houseboating (sail/power)	38.6	3.8	688.11384	0.000
Heli/cat skiing	18.7	0.3	619.25231	0.000
Hunting	18.9	0.4	610.14179	0.000
Scuba diving	19.0	0.6	559.40778	0.000
Amusement or theme parks	56.9	12.3	545.32492	0.000
Sporting events	48.2	9.4	502.33740	0.000
Snowmobiling	18.6	0.7	499.39154	0.000
Whale watching	39.2	6.1	489.49533	0.000
Bicycling	40.4	6.6	483.87405	0.000
Cross country skiing	20.9	1.3	471.61204	0.000
Hiking/backpacking	59.8	15.8	457.62246	0.000
Native (Indian) cultural sites	61.5	16.9	450.11382	0.000
Exploring backcountry wilderness	51.5	12.0	445.57026	0.000
Camping	48.4	11.2	417.33550	0.000
Golfing	43.7	9.1	416.06743	0.000
Ocean kayaking/canoeing	19.6	1.4	414.61676	0.000
Swimming	61.0	20.0	351.77939	0.000
River canoeing/kayaking/rafting	24.8	3.5	329.23354	0.000
Downhill skiing/snowboarding	34.3	7.3	312.09637	0.000
Zoos, natural displays, gardens	83.6	40.9	279.78747	0.000
Purchasing arts and crafts	64.7	25.8	276.80289	0.000
Historic sites	78.5	37.6	262.32397	0.000
Visiting National/Provincial park	81.5	40.4	260.57121	0.000
Local festivals, fairs, events	42.6	13.4	236.54427	0.000
Wildlife viewing/bird watching	69.1	32.3	223.42295	0.000
Concerts/live theatre	27.1	6.6	202.36055	0.000
Nightlife/entertainment	57.2	24.6	202.05473	0.000
Saltwater fishing	21.5	4.4	194.78728	0.000
Sightseeing in the country (outside city/town)	95.1	61.6	188.15488	0.000
Freshwater fishing	23.8	5.8	179.09285	0.000
Gambling	18.4	3.6	172.09306	0.000
Sightseeing in city/town	94.9	67.0	140.56872	0.000
Art galleries, museums	52.7	26.7	125.18478	0.000
Ocean boating (sail/power)	19.6	5.8	109.04588	0.000
Casual walking	89.1	65.0	100.80793	0.000
Shopping	92.5	69.9	97.25924	0.000
Photography	66.8	45.3	70.65499	0.000
Dining out in restaurants	90.2	73.6	56.30906	0.000

TABLE 6. Differentiating Non-Resident BC Trip Element Satisfaction Levels

Trip Elements Assessed	Mean Response*		t	Sig.
	Visited Wineries	Did Not Visit Wineries		
Your overall trip experience	3.80	3.83	−1.109	0.268
Ease of getting to BC	3.41	3.72	−10.373	0.000
Attractions/culture/events	3.55	3.69	−4.859	0.000
City activities	3.37	3.52	−4.102	0.000
Restaurants	3.35	3.48	−4.017	0.000
Value for money	3.32	3.41	−2.603	0.009
Accommodations	3.51	3.58	−2.024	0.043

*Mean responses are sorted in descending order of t value. Satisfaction ratings based on a scale ranging from 1 = not at all satisfied to 4 = very satisfied. The higher the mean score, the higher is the level of satisfaction.

range of scenic, environmentally clean regions. During their travels, they sought opportunities to interact with friendly and hospitable people in relaxing and safe contexts. As a group, they placed less importance than did their Immersionist counterparts on pursuing daring, adventuresome or cultural/heritage activities (Table 9).

Immersionists

Immersionists constituted the remaining 40% of the non-resident wine tourism market. Like their Generalist counterparts, their strongest travel motivations were linked to being able to visit scenic, environmentally clean and safe regions where they could interact in a relaxing fashion with friendly local people. However, they placed greater importance than Generalists on being able to increase their knowledge of the region they were visiting and becoming immersed in a variety of activities. Overall, Immersionists were significantly more emphatic in identifying the importance of natural environments, personal and social discovery, and physical activity as being central to their travel motivations (Table 9).

Other Differentiating Characteristics

Beyond trip motivation characteristics, these two market niches exhibited several other differentiating traits. These were related to socio-demographic, travel philosophy, trip behavior, activity, and product importance-performance characteristics.

TABLE 7. Differentiating Non-Resident Activity Satisfaction Levels

Activities Assessed	Mean Response*		t	Sig.
	Visited Wineries	Did Not Visit Wineries		
Zoos, natural displays, gardens	2.92	3.74	−19.966	0.000
Native (Indian) cultural sites	2.45	3.45	−16.704	0.000
Bicycling	1.87	3.49	−16.317	0.000
Downhill skiing/snowboarding	2.46	3.80	−16.128	0.000
Whale watching	1.72	3.32	−16.035	0.000
Hiking/backpacking	2.64	3.60	−15.560	0.000
Ocean boating (sail/power)	2.02	3.69	−15.356	0.000
Amusement or theme parks	2.39	3.51	−15.342	0.000
Historic sites	2.79	3.50	−14.401	0.000
Sporting events	2.49	3.55	−14.261	0.000
Concerts/live theatre	1.98	3.37	−13.651	0.000
Lake boating (sail/power)	1.74	3.37	−13.574	0.000
Wildlife viewing/bird watching	2.82	3.52	−13.452	0.000
Freshwater fishing	1.84	3.35	−12.947	0.000
Visiting National/Provincial park	3.37	3.80	−12.914	0.000
Saltwater fishing	1.73	3.37	−12.621	0.000
Exploring backcountry wilderness	2.83	3.61	−11.467	0.000
Art galleries, museums	2.81	3.50	−10.884	0.000
River canoeing/kayaking/rafting	2.10	3.63	−10.684	0.000
Shopping	2.94	3.34	−10.515	0.000
Swimming	2.98	3.57	−10.451	0.000
Purchasing arts and crafts	2.84	3.33	−8.818	0.000
Horseback riding	2.02	3.16	−8.709	0.000
Cross country skiing	1.76	3.34	−8.400	0.000
Sightseeing in the country (outside city/town)	3.50	3.74	−8.262	0.000
Ocean kayaking/canoeing	1.75	3.38	−8.225	0.000
Local festivals, fairs, events	2.79	3.42	−8.178	0.000
Golfing	2.92	3.61	−7.834	0.000
Sightseeing in city/town	3.29	3.52	−6.681	0.000
Camping	3.16	3.65	−6.607	0.000
Photography	3.34	3.58	−6.451	0.000
Snowmobiling	1.71	3.35	−6.266	0.000
Casual walking	3.47	3.65	−5.940	0.000
Dining out in restaurants	3.26	3.40	−3.986	0.000
Lake house boating	2.39	3.15	−3.591	0.000
Hunting	1.89	2.74	−2.211	0.030

*Mean responses are sorted in descending order of t value. Satisfaction ratings based on a scale ranging from 1 = not at all satisfied to 4 = very satisfied. The higher the mean, the higher is the level of satisfaction.

TABLE 8. Differentiating Non-Resident Destination Selection Factor Satisfaction Levels

	Mean Response*			
Destination Selection Factors Assessed	**Visited Wineries**	**Did Not Visit Wineries**	**t**	**Sig.**
Indulging in luxury such as staying in first class hotels	2.44	3.24	−11.095	0.000
Doing daring and adventuresome activities	2.47	3.24	−10.066	0.000
Going to a place that is good for the family	3.44	3.71	−8.387	0.000
Getting a good currency exchange rate	3.05	3.45	−8.177	0.000
Going to places with friendly and hospitable people	3.41	3.66	−7.990	0.000
Having the opportunity to shop	2.95	3.29	−7.714	0.000
Learning about Native (Indian) culture and art	2.74	3.20	−7.132	0.000
Being physically active	3.35	3.56	−5.945	0.000
Participating in outdoor activities	3.41	3.63	−5.922	0.000
Visiting wilderness and undisturbed areas	3.14	3.44	−5.691	0.000
Travelling to places where I feel safe and secure	3.52	3.66	−4.387	0.000
Visiting historic sites or areas	3.45	3.62	−4.326	0.000
Visiting attractions such as museums, art galleries, zoos, etc.	3.15	3.38	−4.319	0.000
Experiencing and seeing a coastal area	3.49	3.66	−3.921	0.000
Getting to know local people	3.00	3.18	−3.740	0.000
Visiting clean cities and towns	3.71	3.59	3.519	0.000
Attending sporting events	3.22	2.93	3.222	0.001
Experiencing and seeing a mountain area	3.81	3.71	3.128	0.002
Resting and relaxing	3.59	3.68	−2.944	0.003
Visiting a place that takes good care of its environment	3.66	3.56	2.677	0.007
Going to places I've heard about from friends or relatives	3.45	3.55	−2.578	0.010
Having a variety of things to see and do	3.65	3.56	2.557	0.011

*Mean responses are sorted in descending order by absolute magnitude of the t value. Satisfaction ratings based on a scale ranging from 1 = not at all satisfied to 4 = very satisfied. The higher the mean, the higher is the level of satisfaction.

Socio-Demographic Characteristics

When compared with Generalists, Immersionists were more apt to be younger and less formally educated. As a group, significantly greater proportions of them were fully employed and female (Table 10).

Travel Philosophies

Compared to Immersionists, Generalists were significantly more inclined to take leisure trips that were of greater frequency but shorter in duration. They also were significantly more apt to pursue holidays

TABLE 9. Differentiating Non-Resident Niche Market Travel Motivations

Destination Selection Factors Assessed	Mean Response*		t	Sig.
	Generalists	Immersionists		
Visiting wilderness and undisturbed areas	1.70	3.28	-14.02052	0.00000
Experiencing and seeing a coastal area	2.02	3.66	-12.58880	0.00000
Learning new things, increasing my knowledge	2.43	3.68	-10.97962	0.00000
Visiting historic sites or areas	1.94	3.19	-10.32683	0.00000
Getting to know local people	2.12	3.25	-10.12584	0.00000
Viewing wildlife and birds	2.31	3.45	-9.91257	0.00000
Learning about Native (Indian) culture and art	1.51	2.63	-9.52927	0.00000
Experiencing and seeing a mountain area	2.99	3.86	-8.67409	0.00000
Visiting a place that takes good care of its environment	2.95	3.86	-8.31191	0.00000
Visiting attractions such as museums, art galleries, zoos, etc.	2.26	3.08	-7.79351	0.00000
Being physically active	2.48	3.44	-7.69034	0.00000
Visiting cities and/or towns	2.53	3.36	-7.43444	0.00000
Having a variety of things to see and do	2.86	3.73	-7.38080	0.00000
Going to place I've heard about from friends or relatives	2.40	3.23	-6.69181	0.00000
Visiting clean cities and towns	3.08	3.78	-6.69088	0.00000
Visiting scenic areas	3.31	3.89	-6.64454	0.00000
Going to a place that is good for the family	2.59	3.60	-6.64211	0.00000
Visiting places with unique and interesting restaurants	2.57	3.35	-6.36249	0.00000
Travelling to places where I feel safe and secure	3.03	3.78	-6.34166	0.00000
Getting a good currency exchange rate	2.28	3.17	-6.13401	0.00000
Having the opportunity to shop	2.40	3.11	-5.86661	0.00000
Highway transportation within BC	2.76	3.47	-5.74514	0.00000
Getting value for the cost of the trip	3.09	3.67	-5.49804	0.00000
Going to places with friendly and hospitable people	3.14	3.73	-4.98580	0.00000
Doing daring and adventuresome activities	1.56	2.12	-4.71606	0.00000
Enjoying night life and entertainment	1.76	2.35	-4.69335	0.00000
Ease of getting to BC	2.87	3.45	-4.60591	0.00001
Attending sporting events	1.69	2.26	-4.53134	0.00001
Indulging in luxury such as staying in first class hotels	1.69	2.22	-4.07925	0.00006
Air access within BC	1.52	2.04	-3.70122	0.00027
Participating in outdoor activities	2.68	3.13	-3.36911	0.00088
Visiting a place where people speak my language	2.90	3.36	-3.24446	0.00134

*Mean responses are sorted in descending order of t values. Importance scores based on a scale ranging from 1 = not at all important to 4 = very important. The higher the mean, the higher is the level of importance placed on the destination selection factors.

TABLE 10. Most Frequently Reported Market Niche Socio-Demographic Characteristics

Characteristic	Generalists	Immersionists
Education	College/university degree (31.1%)	College/university degree (32.4%)
Employment Status	Self-employed (29.4%)	Employed full time (39.3%)
Gender	Female (51.1%)	Female (56.1%)
Total Annual Household Income	$100,000 or over (25.3%)	$100,000 or over (23.8%)
Average Age	43.6	39.0

which were prearranged in advance. On the other hand, Immersionists were more likely to partake in vacations that incorporated guided tours (Table 11).

Travel Characteristics

Immersionists were quite different from Generalists with respect to their travel patterns. In particular, Immersionists were generally less familiar with BC as a vacation destination. However, upon arriving, they stayed significantly longer in the province. In addition, despite travelling in smaller travel parties than their Generalist counterparts, they spent significantly more than them (Table 12).

Trip Activities

Immersionists were much more active than Generalists with respect to their incidences of participation in a range of trip activities. They had higher levels of participation in all of the 40 trip activities examined. Their overall levels of involvement were significantly higher than those of Generalists in 43% of these pursuits (Table 13).

Trip Satisfaction Levels

Compared to their Generalist counterparts, Immersionists were more satisfied with their overall trip experience in BC. They were significantly more pleased with the attractions/culture/events they experienced on their trips than were Generalists (Table 14).

TABLE 11. Differentiating Market Niche Travel Philosophies

Travel Philosophy	Mean Response *		t	Sig.
	Generalists	Immersionists		
I prefer to go on guided tours when vacationing	1.80	2.15	−3.12472	0.00201
In any one year I would rather take a number of short vacations instead of one long vacation	2.98	2.68	2.59969	0.00993
I like to have all my travel arrangements made before I start out on my trip	3.04	2.83	2.00433	0.04619

*Mean responses are sorted in descending order of absolute magnitude of the t value. Philosophy scores based on a scale ranging from 1 = strongly disagree to 4 = strongly agree. The higher the mean score, the higher is the level of agreement with the travel philosophy.

TABLE 12. Differentiating Market Niche Travel Characteristics and Expenditures

Trip Characteristics	Mean Response		t	Sig.
	Generalists	Immersionists		
Trips taken for leisure to B.C. in the past three years	3.04	2.17	2.91740	0.00392
Length of stay in BC	9.62	12.01	−2.20140	0.02869
Total household trip expenditures within BC (dollars) *	932.33	2,158.18	−5.85201	0.00000

*All expenditures are in Canadian dollars and include taxes.

Activity Satisfaction Levels

Immersionists expressed higher levels of satisfaction with the activities they participated in than did Generalists. This was most apparent with respect to photography, visiting native cultural sites, dining out/nightlife and entertainment and visiting national/provincial parks. Generalists, on the other hand, expressed higher levels of satisfaction with the pursuits of golfing and other sporting events than did their Immersionist counterparts (Table 15).

Service and Facility Satisfaction Levels

For the most part, Immersionists tended to express higher levels of satisfaction with destination selection factors than did their Generalist counterparts. This was particularly true with respect to experiencing and seeing BC's mountainous areas, unique and interesting restaurants, cities and towns, shopping and the variety of alternatives available to visitors.

TABLE 13. Differentiating Market Niche Activity Characteristics

Activities Pursued	Percentage of Respondents		χ^2	Sig.
	Generalists	Immersionists		
Historic sites	62.6	89.6	21.604	0.000
Exploring backcountry wilderness	32.9	58.8	15.915	0.000
Hiking/backpacking	45.6	71.1	15.470	0.000
Zoos, natural displays, gardens	68.0	89.6	15.030	0.000
Camping	30.8	53.6	12.617	0.000
Native (Indian) cultural sites	42.5	65.6	12.439	0.000
Swimming	45.6	64.6	8.422	0.004
Lake boating (sail/power)	20.5	37.5	8.391	0.004
Snowmobiling	16.4	32.3	8.288	0.004
Amusement or theme parks	41.5	58.3	6.594	0.010
Whale watching	27.2	42.7	6.276	0.012
Sightseeing in city/town	91.8	99.0	5.817	0.016
River canoeing/kayaking/rafting	22.4	35.4	4.890	0.027
Downhill skiing/snowboarding	19.9	32.3	4.798	0.028
Visiting National/Provincial park	72.6	84.5	4.740	0.029
Shopping	87.0	94.8	3.950	0.047
Saltwater fishing	21.9	33.3	3.880	0.049

TABLE 14. Differentiating Market Niche Trip Element Satisfaction Levels

Item	Mean Response*		t	Sig.
	Generalists	Immersionists		
Your overall trip experience	3.71	3.83	−1.83920	0.06719
Attractions/culture/events	3.53	3.70	−2.10301	0.03672

*Mean satisfaction scores based on a scale ranging from 1 = strongly disagree to 4 = strongly agree. The higher the mean, the higher is the level of satisfaction with the trip elements.

Generalists expressed higher levels of satisfaction with opportunities to indulge in luxury, the nightlife and entertainment offerings, attending sporting events and doing adventuresome activities (Table 16).

DESTINATION IMPORTANCE-PERFORMANCE COMPARISONS

Distinctive gaps in the IPA ratings of destination attributes were apparent for both Generalist and Immersionist respondents. Generalists

TABLE 15. Differentiating Market Niche Activity Satisfaction Levels

Activities Assessed	Mean Response*		t	Sig.
	Generalists	Immersionists		
Photography	3.09	3.77	-4.93962	0.00000
Native (Indian) cultural sites	2.23	3.00	-3.96607	0.00012
Dining out in restaurants	3.10	3.42	-3.46288	0.00064
Visiting National/Provincial park	3.26	3.72	3.32681	0.00106
Golfing	2.90	2.01	3.14936	0.00223
Nightlife/entertainment	2.58	3.06	-2.68407	0.00820
Sporting events	2.73	2.12	2.41248	0.01767
Snowmobiling	1.52	2.32	-2.39239	0.02029
Sightseeing in city/town	3.33	3.53	-2.08064	0.03858
Local festivals, fairs, events	2.63	3.08	-2.06030	0.04181
Sightseeing in the country (outside city/town)	3.51	3.73	-2.04128	0.04238

*Mean responses are sorted in descending order by absolute magnitude of the t value. Satisfaction scores based on a scale ranging from 1 = not at all satisfied to 4 = very satisfied. The higher the mean, the higher is the level of satisfaction with the activities.

TABLE 16. Differentiating Market Niche Destination Selection Factor Satisfaction Levels

Item	Mean Response *		t	Sig.
	Generalists	Immersionists		
Experiencing and seeing a mountain area	3.55	3.88	-4.17119	0.00004
Visiting places with unique and interesting restaurants	3.08	3.48	-4.00990	0.00009
Visiting cities and/or towns	3.21	3.56	-3.68703	0.00029
Indulging in luxury such as staying in first class hotels	3.30	2.70	3.24438	0.00173
Having the opportunity to shop	3.09	3.41	-2.76511	0.00626
Enjoying night life and entertainment	3.22	2.76	2.58751	0.01104
Visiting a place where people speak my language	3.50	3.77	-2.54494	0.01176
Attending sporting events	3.27	2.76	2.47913	0.01538
Having a variety of things to see and do	3.44	3.64	-2.36516	0.01902
Viewing wildlife and birds	3.31	3.55	-2.33917	0.02055
Visiting a place that takes good care of its environment	3.42	3.65	-2.33263	0.02069
Doing daring and adventuresome activities	3.23	2.87	2.09039	0.03919
Getting to know local people	3.22	3.43	-1.98473	0.04882

*Mean responses are sorted in descending order by absolute magnitude of the t value. Satisfaction scores are based on a scale ranging from 1 = not at all satisfied to 4 = very satisfied. In other words, the higher the mean, the higher is the level of satisfaction.

were more satisfied than were Immersionists with those attributes they considered important in their selection of travel destinations. Overall, their satisfaction with each destination selection feature examined was higher than the corresponding level of importance they attached to that attribute.

Destination selection features that received highest satisfaction ratings in the minds of the Generalists and were also relatively high on their importance ratings were related to opportunities to enjoy scenic areas, as well as clean and safe communities with hospitable people (Table 17). Important attributes which elicited particularly poor satisfaction evaluations were associated with providing opportunities to pursue more outdoor oriented and other adventuresome pursuits in high quality natural and cultural environments. Overall, Generalists were seeking more features which added value to their experience through activities that afforded them opportunities to increase their knowledge and interaction with local people (Figure 1).

Generally, Immersionists expressed less satisfaction than did their Generalist counterparts with those regional attributes they considered most important to their selection of a travel destination. Only one of the ten most important destination selection factors identified by Immersionists received mean satisfaction scores as good or better than their corresponding importance ratings (Table 18).

TABLE 17. Generalists' Destination Selection Factor Importance-Performance Gaps

Destination Selection Factor	Mean Response*		Difference
	Importance	Performance	
Participating in outdoor activities	3.31	3.43	0.12
Visiting scenic areas	3.21	3.73	0.52
Doing daring and adventuresome activities	3.14	3.23	0.09
Getting value for the cost of the trip	3.09	3.37	0.28
Visiting clean cities and towns	3.08	3.56	0.48
Travelling to places where I feel safe and secure	3.03	3.52	0.49
Viewing wildlife and birds	2.99	3.31	0.32
Going to places with friendly and hospitable people	2.97	3.62	0.65
Visiting a place that takes good care of its environment	2.95	3.42	0.47
Visiting a place where people speak my language	2.90	3.50	0.60

*Mean responses are sorted in descending order of importance based on a scale ranging from 1 = not at all satisfied to 4 = very satisfied. In other words, the higher the mean, the higher is the level of satisfaction.

FIGURE 1. Generalists' Destination Selection Factor Importance-Performance Analysis

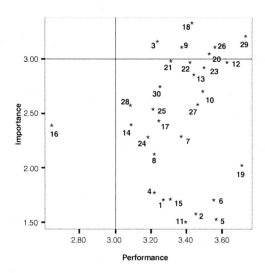

Legend:

Key	Variable
1	Attending sporting events
2	Being physically active
3	Doing daring and adventuresome activities
4	Enjoying night life and entertainment
5	Experiencing and seeing a coastal area
6	Experiencing and seeing a mountain area
7	Getting a good currency exchange rate
8	Getting to know local people
9	Getting value for the cost of the trip
10	Going to a place that is good for the family
11	Going to place I've heard about from friends or relatives
12	Going to places with friendly and hospitable people
13	Having a variety of things to see and do
14	Having the opportunity to shop
15	Indulging in luxury such as staying in first class hotels

Key	Variable
16	Learning about Native (Indian) culture and art
17	Learning new things, increasing my knowledge
18	Participating in outdoor activities
19	Resting and relaxing
20	Travelling to places where I feel safe and secure
21	Viewing wildlife and birds
22	Visiting a place that takes good care of its environment
23	Visiting a place where people speak my language
24	Visiting attractions such as museums, art galleries, zoos, etc.
25	Visiting cities and/or towns
26	Visiting clean cities and towns
27	Visiting historic sites or areas
28	Visiting places with unique and interesting restaurants.
29	Visiting scenic areas
30	Visiting wilderness and undistubed areas

TABLE 18. Immersionists' Destination Selection Factor Importance-Performance Gaps

Destination Selection Factor	Mean Response*		Difference
	Importance	Performance	
Participating in outdoor activities	3.89	3.32	0.57
Viewing wildlife and birds	3.86	3.55	0.31
Visiting a place that takes good care of its environment	3.86	3.65	0.21
Travelling to places where I feel safe and secure	3.78	3.59	0.19
Visiting clean cities and towns	3.78	3.64	0.14
Doing daring and adventuresome activities	3.73	2.87	0.86
Having a variety of things to see and do	3.73	3.64	0.09
Learning new things, increasing my knowledge	3.68	3.28	0.40
Getting value for the cost of the trip	3.67	3.53	0.14
Resting and relaxing	3.66	3.83	0.17

*Mean responses are sorted in descending order of importance based on a scale ranging from 1 = not at all satisfied to 4 = very satisfied. In other words, the higher the mean, the higher is the level of satisfaction.

Important destination features for which Immersionists expressed considerable satisfaction were associated with opportunities to experience well-managed safe, scenic, and natural areas with wildlife. Key destination attributes which failed to measure up to satisfaction expectations of these Immersionists were tied to limited opportunities to experience more culturally and socially interactive adventures involving local people and undisturbed places (Figure 2).

MANAGEMENT IMPLICATIONS

It is apparent that BC wine tourism product and market development for non-resident markets are in their early infancy. There is neither high levels of market penetration nor strong satisfaction associated with those destination selection factors important to them. To address these deficiencies, greater focus should be placed on accommodating the needs of the Generalist and Immersionists in both product development and marketing initiatives.

Product Development Strategies

To achieve greater levels of visitor satisfaction, a range of product development initiatives should be considered. These are discussed in the following paragraphs.

FIGURE 2. Immersionists' Destination Selection Factor Importance-Performance Analysis

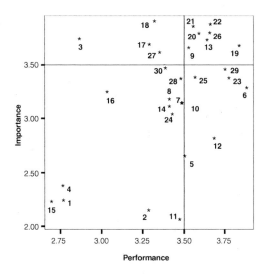

Legend:

Key	Variable	Key	Variable
1	Attending sporting events	16	Learning about Native (Indian) culture and art
2	Being physically active	17	Learning new things, increasing my knowledge
3	Doing daring and adventuresome activities	18	Participating in outdoor activities
4	Enjoying night life and entertainment	19	Resting and relaxing
5	Experiencing and seeing a coastal area	20	Travelling to places where I feel safe and secure
6	Experiencing and seeing a mountain area	21	Viewing wildlife and birds
7	Getting a good currency exchange rate	22	Visiting a place that takes good care of its environment
8	Getting to know local people	23	Visiting a place where people speak my language
9	Getting value for the cost of the trip	24	Visiting attractions such as museums, art galleries, zoos, etc.
10	Going to a place that is good for the family	25	Visiting cities and/or towns
11	Going to place I've heard about from friends or relatives	26	Visiting clean cities and towns
12	Going to places with friendly and hospitable people	27	Visiting historic sites or areas
13	Having a variety of things to see and do	28	Visiting places with unique and interesting restaurants
14	Having the opportunity to shop	29	Visiting scenic areas
15	Indulging in luxury such as staying in first class hotels	30	Visiting wilderness and undisturbed areas

Broadening the Wine Tourism Experience

Both Generalists and Immersionists want more value-added dimensions incorporated into their wine country travel. The added value they are seeking is linked to more humanistic, experiential and educative experiences that extend beyond simply consuming wine to encompassing a more integrated range of leisure activities. Added value winery experiences of interest to these markets include a variety of restaurants, cafes, tours, accommodation, events and education programs which can contribute to their general life experiences. For the Immersionists, good food and interactive attractions such as well interpreted natural areas and unique craft/art galleries can play an important role in reinforcing the image of wine as a lifestyle product. For Generalists, incorporating festivals, concerts and events into the wine country experience provides a means of diversifying their activity options within their more general travel agendas. The creation of regional cuisine and the development of cooking schools by wineries and restaurateurs can further broaden the market base for both Immersionists and Generalists.

For the most part, such product development opportunities reach well beyond the capabilities of individual wineries, and extend into the realm of many tourism and hospitality providers. The province's wine and tourism industries would benefit significantly from pursuing strategic alliances with each other in such product development initiatives.

Protecting and Managing Access to Regional Natural and Cultural Resources

Natural and cultural landscapes should be recognized as integral if not central components of the tourism asset base in wine tourism regions. Non-resident wine tourists cite the importance of opportunities to pursue their leisure experiences within well maintained natural and heritage environs. While "winescapes" are often romanticized as areas encompassing the "rural idyll," they are frequently subject to the challenges of land use conflicts associated with residential, tourism development and viticulture expansion (Carlsen & Dowling, 2001). Conserving the natural resource base in wine regions is a product development function that requires the collaboration and sound planning of many partners. Individual wineries must take a lead in protecting and conserving the key resources they use, but the policies of communities and tourism associations must also foster and support such practices.

Implementing Customer Service Training

One of the most revealing traits of non-resident wine tourists discovered in this study is that many of them are destination-naïve travellers. As such, these visitors probably require considerably more information and support from a visitor management perspective than do other visitors to the province. To reduce any intimidation or constraint that they may feel with respect to visiting the province's emerging wine tourism destinations, providing guidance and information should extend from their point of initial contact for trip planning through to on-going customer service during site visits.

Customer service training programs designed to increase the responsiveness of wine tourism destination suppliers to the needs of non-resident travellers should be developed. Such programs might focus on strengthening the ability of wine and tourism suppliers to inform tourists of the array of natural and cultural destination activities that can be linked together to create customized and satisfying wine country experiences. Information concerning the availability and appropriateness of local and regional entertainment, crafts and souvenirs, accommodation, cellar door tasting sites, quality wines, winery tours, art galleries, cultural landmarks, scenic viewpoints, and bike routes for wine country holiday adventures should be made readily available to all service providers for dissemination to Generalists and Immersionists visiting wine tourism destinations. Currently knowledge of such information is quite limited amongst tourism and wine industry service providers and is not readily accessible to non-resident wine tourists.

Market Development

Existing literature suggests that many opportunities exist to expand the size of the non-resident wine tourist market for the province. However, this expansion will not occur without significant commitments to the strategic marketing of wine tourism in high potential markets. The following sections suggest various strategies for attracting more non-resident wine tourists to the province.

Developing Strategic Marketing Alliances

The tourism and wine industries have much to gain from forming strategic marketing alliances. From a communication perspective, incorporating winery related products and services into the province's tourism marketing mix will help to: fortify the region's current market position which builds on images of natural and idyll landscapes; diversify its portfolio of cultural and natural tourism products that are clearly central to the province and region's positioning; attract non-resident Generalist and Immersionist markets that have only been partially accessed; and gain access to non-resident markets that will travel to the province during underutilized portions of the year.

Similarly, wine industry alliances with the tourism industry can help to broaden non-resident awareness and customer confidence in the quality of BC wines. Combining the resources of both sectors in market development and promotional activities will also assist in extending the reach and effectiveness of available but limited marketing resources in both industries. Currently, efforts to develop such inter-industry marketing alliances are limited in BC.

Developing Customized Packages

Generalist wine tourists in particular are seeking travel experiences that can be planned in advance, are filled with activities, and are responsive to evolving travel circumstances. Immersionist wine tourists place importance on having access to well orchestrated guided tours. Wine and tourism industry organizations need to cooperatively develop "customized and self-selecting" packages of products and services which can be created and booked in a "no hassle" fashion. Central to such packages are mechanisms that increase consumer awareness of regional wine products. Australia's Tourism Victoria and the Australian Tourism Commission have developed many initiatives designed to make reservation bookings and touring easier for the visitor. They have also created a program that includes promoting Australia via improved winery information, tasting notes, tourism maps of wine regions, posted hours of operation, restaurant guides serving quality domestic wine, and accommodation directories in wine country. Such initiatives have not yet emerged to the same extent in a BC wine tourism context.

Developing Wine Festivals and Events

Special events, such as community wine festivals or concerts at wineries can add considerably to wine country tourism experiences. They can also enhance awareness of wine products and services for both Immersionist and Generalist markets. Such events can draw consumers to wine destinations at off-peak periods of the wine production and tourism seasons, and heighten awareness of regional attractions and services. They can also create market-positioning benefits for wine producers and tourism businesses.

In the Napa Valley region of California, a series of seasonal wine festivals is provided for resident and non-resident wine visitors. During these events, a diverse range of activities and wine products are promoted. These include elaborate wine tastings, intimate vineyard luncheons, full gourmet and wine-matched dinners, informative wine tours and demonstrations and wine cooking seminars. In combination they are used to raise awareness levels of this destination area for travellers, as well as promote the region's wine products. The full potential of such festivals and events has only partially been realized in BC.

Incorporating "Winescape" Imagery

From a market positioning perspective, alliances between tourism and the BC wine industry might initially focus on incorporating "winescape" imagery into the marketing of the province. BC has a well-developed and positive position in its key international markets. This position is linked to images of outdoor and nature-based adventure tourism experiences–both of which are important to Generalist and Immersion market niches. The addition of spectacular rural "winescapes" imagery will add an appealing and complementary cultural dimension to the overall attractiveness of the province amongst non-resident Immersionist wine tourists. This could help to raise consumer awareness of the expanding diversity of complementary tourism product options available in the province. It might also assist in positioning the wine industry's products clearly within the very credible and recognized Super Natural British Columbia travel brand. Currently, such imagery and positioning is not on the "radar screen" of most non-resident travelers visiting the province.

Developing a Common Brand

Because so many wine operations are relatively small in size, it is often necessary for them to develop alliances to create the critical mass needed to gain a significant market presence. This is especially the case in BC, where most of the wineries are farm gate or estate wineries. Marketing brand alliances occur in many other wine regions, and provide a sense of brand identity in the marketplace. In France, some wine regions and communities have invested heavily in infra-

structure, including museums, research centers, restaurants, accommodation and workshops to create a distinct market brand (Thevenin,
1996). In other cases, associations or clubs of wine growers such as the
Great Wine Club of the Chateaux of Languedoc have come together to
market wine trips and vacations to tourists under a common wine country vacation brand. France's Alsace region has 85 wine visitor sites and
12 wine museums, many of which are connected by a wine road
(Choisy, 1996).

Branded wine tour routes offer an effective means of bringing varying wineries and other tourism services together to create a whole that is
often greater than the sum of its parts. Wine roads (or routes) have been
created throughout Europe (e.g., Germany, France, but Italy is still
planning them), South Africa, the US and Canada (e.g., wineroute.com;
bcwine.com). Other wine regions have developed wine routes for lei-
surely train and bicycle travel. Often these routes provide accompany-
ing transportation vehicles, which carry wines purchased by travelers
back to the visitors' places of accommodation. Making these "friendly"
for various forms of leisure travel is critical in creating a sense of
no-hassle access for Immersionist wine tourists and Generalists interested in enjoying their wine country experience. Such branding is only
in its infancy in BC.

CONCLUSIONS

The overriding hypothesis examined in this paper was that non-resident wine tourists exhibited travel attitudes and behaviors, which
clearly distinguished them from other non-resident visitors to the province. Based on the this investigation it was clear that not only were wine
tourists distinctive from other visitors to BC with respect to their travel
characteristics and preferences, but there were also relatively unique
Generalist and Immersionist sub-segments within the non-resident
wine market itself. While there were many commonalties in the traits of
these market niches, it was clear that each wine tourist segment placed
varying levels of importance and satisfaction on those destination features critical to the enjoyment of their trip. Their attitudes about the importance and performance of these destination attributes provided the
basis for recommending several overriding wine tourism product and
marketing strategies for BC.

Attracting and holding these non-resident visitors to BC wine producing regions requires the combined and coordinated efforts of both

wine and tourism industry stakeholders. The need for these stake-holders to work together is punctuated by the fact that most wineries in BC are limited in their physical capacity to manage large numbers of tourists on-site, and constrained in their access to the technical and financial resources needed to market their products and services to non-resident visitors.

Non-resident travellers can add an exciting and rewarding dimension to the market mix of both wine and tourism stakeholders in BC destination regions if the "wine country experience" is well organized and clearly marketed. However, successful retention of non-resident markets will depend to a large extent on how well the product expectations and needs of these markets are understood and incorporated into future product development initiatives. This research suggests that many tourists are seeking more than the taste of a quality vintage when they visit "wine country." Rather, their travel motivations centre around experiencing idyllic natural landscapes; discovering interesting and different cultures, heritages and lifestyles; and enjoying interactions with friendly and informed local people. All of these elements, when combined with visits to attractive wineries create a fine blend for a growing number of non-resident tourists. This paper helps to provide a better understanding of the relationship between the products the wine industry produces and the experiences that wine tourists expect. However, to consolidate and fortify destination management organization understanding of the nature of this relationship, at least three key research themes should be encouraged.

First, more investigations should focus on identifying the characteristics of sub-groups of wine tourists. While much of the current research focuses on gathering data concerning traditional traits of consumer behavior, there is a need to focus greater attention on identifying those experiential attributes which bind the various physical components of the wine tourism experience together.

Second, there is a need to focus more research on the role and management of the settings in which wine tourism occurs. Existing research clearly identifies the importance of scenic natural areas, healthy flora and fauna, and interesting rural cultural environments as settings for wine tourism experiences. However, little of this research examines how these features should be incorporated into the planning and management of wine tourism regions. More must be done to determine those policies and programs, which will protect the natural and heritage backdrop against which wine tourism occurs.

Finally, more research should focus on ways of enhancing the social and cultural dimensions of wine tourism. Discovering quaint and ideally authentic places, as well as socializing with local personalities in wine country, are considered priorities for many wine tourism travellers. Through these interactions, visitors can gain a cultural sense of a place, so crucial to many visitor expectations. Research should focus on determining the most sensitive and effective means of facilitating interactions between visitors and other elements of the wine tourism experience (e.g., cuisine, festivals, cultural attractions, accommodation, tours, information centres, wine tastings, etc.). More targeted consumer research, which explores the detailed destination expectations and product preferences of such wine tourists, would provide a useful information base on which to explore this issue.

REFERENCES

Beverland, M., James, K., Porter, C., & Stace, G. (1998). Wine tourists–missed opportunities in West Auckland. *Australian and New Zealand Wine Industry Journal*, 13(4): 403-407.

BCWI. (1998). *Annual report 1997/98.* Kelowna: BC Wine Institute.

BCWI. (1998/99). *Wine Institute annual report 1998/99.* Kelowna: BC Wine Institute.

BCWI. (1999). *Annual Report 1999.* Kelowna: BC Wine Institute.

Carlsen, J., & Dowling, R. (2001). Regional wine tourism: A plan of development for Western Australia. *Tourism Recreation Research*, 26(20): 45-52.

Choisy, C. (1996). Lepoinds du tourisme viti-vinicole. *Espaces*, 140: 30-33.

Chon K.S., Weaver, P.A., & Kim, C.Y. (1988). Marketing your community: Image analysis in Norfolk. *Cornell Hotel-Restaurant Quarterly*, 31(4): 31-37.

Crompton, J.L., & MacKay, K.J. (1988). Users' perceptions the relative importance of service quality dimensions in selected recreation programs. *Leisure Sciences*, 11: 367-375.

Crompton, J.L., MacKay, K.J., & Fesenmaier, D.R. (1991). Identifying dimensions of service quality in public recreation. *Journal of Park and Recreation Administration*, 9(3):15-27.

Dodd, T. (1995). Opportunities and pitfalls of tourism in a developing wine industry. *International Journal of Wine Marketing*, 7(1): 5-16.

Dodd, T.H. & Bigotte, V. (1995). *Visitors to Texas wineries: Their demographic characteristics and purchasing behavior.* Lubbock, TX: Texas Wine Marketing Research Institute.

Folwell, R., & Grassell, B. (1989). Characteristics of tasting rooms in Washington wineries. *Research Bulletin XB 1013*. Pullman, WA: College of Agriculture and Home Economics Research Centre, Washington State University.

Getz, D. (1999). Global overview and perspective on development. In R. Dowling & J. Carlsen (Eds.), *Wine Tourism: Perfect Partners. Proceedings of the First Austra-*

lian *Wine Tourism Conference, May 1998, Margaret River, Western Australia* (pp. 13-34). Perth: Edith Cowan University.

Hall, C.M., Sharples, L., Cambourne, B., & Macionis, N. (Eds.) (2000). *Wine Tourism Around the World: Development, Management and Markets.* Oxford: Butterworth-Heinemann.

Hansen, E., & Bush, R.J. (1999). Understanding customer quality requirements: Model and application. *Industrial Marketing Management*, 28(2): 119-130.

Howat, G., Absher, J.D., Crilley, C., & Milne, I. (1996). Measuring customer service quality in sports and leisure centers, *Managing Leisure*, 1: 77-89.

Hudson, S., & Shephard, G.W.H. (1998). Measuring service quality at tourism destinations: An application of importance performance analysis to an alpine ski resort. *Journal of Tourism Marketing*, 7(3): 61-77.

Johnson, G. (1998). *Wine tourism in New Zealand–A national survey of wineries.* Unpublished Dip. Tour. Dissertation. University of Otago.

King, C., & Morris R. (1997). To taste or not to taste: To charge or not to charge. *Wine Industry Journal*, 12(4): 381-384.

Kuss, F.R., Graefe, A.R., & Vaske, J. J. (1990). *Visitor Impact Management: A Review of Research.* Volume 1. Washington, DC: National Parks and Conservation Association.

Lawson, R., Thyne, M., & Young, T. (1997). *New Zealand Holidays: A Travel Lifestyles Study.* Dunedin: Department of Marketing, University of Otago.

Longo, A.M. (1999). *Wine tourism in New Zealand: An exploration of the characteristics and motivations of winery visitors.* Unpublished Dip. Tour. Dissertation. University of Otago.

Machin, R. (2000). *Quaffing through the Bay: An examination of wine tourism in Hawkes Bay.* Unpublished Dip. Tour. Dissertation, University of Otago, New Zealand.

Maddern, C., & Golledge, S. (1996). *Victorian Wineries Tourism Council Cellar Door Survey.* Victoria Wineries Tourism Council.

Martilla, J.A., & James, J.C. (1977). Importance-performance analysis. *Journal of Marketing*, 41(1): 77-79.

Mitchell, R. and Hall, C.M. (2001). The influence of gender and region on the New Zealand winery visit. *Tourism Recreation Research*, 26(2): 63-75.

Mitchell, R., Hall, C.M., McIntosh, A., & Johnson, G. (1999). Getting to know the wine the winery visitor. *New Zealand Wine Grower*, 2(3): 25.

MTV (Movimento del Turismo del Vino) (1995). URL: http://ulysees.s.it/mtv/

NZTB (1993). *New Zealand International Visitors Survey 1992/93.* Wellington: New Zealand Tourism Board.

NZTB (1997). *New Zealand International Visitors Survey 1995/96.* Wellington: New Zealand Tourism Board.

O'Neill, M., & Charters, S. (1999). Service quality at the cellar door: Implications for Western Australia's developing wine industry. *Managing Service Quality*, 10(2): 112-122.

Parasuraman, A., Berry, L.L., & Zeithaml, V.A. (1994). SERVQUAL: A multiple-item scale for measuring consumer perceptions of service quality. *Journal of Retailing*, 64(1): 12-40.

Rachman, G. (1999). In a glass. *The Economist*, December, 18, 91-105.

Reilly, A. (1996). *A marketing approach for small winemakers in regional areas*. Unpublished masters thesis, Business Administration, University of Adelaide.

Robins, P. (1999). Potential research into wine tourism. In R.Dowling & J. Carlsen (Eds.), *Wine Tourism: Perfect Partners. Proceedings of the First Australian Wine Tourism Conference, May 1998, Margaret River, Western Australia* (pp. 81-91). Perth: Edith Cowan University.

Sampson, S.E., & Showalter, M.J. (1999). The performance-importance response function: Observations and implications. *The Service Industries Journal*, 19(3): 1-25.

Saunders, D. (1996, August 16). Niagara wine country uncorks a feud. *The Globe and Mail*, p. 1A.

Slack, N. (1994). The importance-performance matrix as a determinant of improvement priority. *International Journal of Operations and Production Management*, 14(5): 59-75.

SATC (1997). *Wine and Tourism: A Background Research Report*. Adelaide: South Australian Tourist Commission.

SPSS (1997). *SPSS Base 7.5 Application Guide*. Toronto: Prentice Hall.

Thevenin, C. (1996). Quands le vignerons font du tourisme. *Espaces*, 140: 43-48.

TBC (2001). *Annual Report*. Victoria: Tourism British Columbia.

TBC (1997). *BC Visitor Study: Report on Travel in British Columbia*. Victoria: Tourism British Columbia.

Vaske, J. J., Beaman, J., Stanley, R. & Genier, M. (1996). Importance-performance and segmentation. *Journal of Travel and Tourism Marketing*, 5(3), 225-240.

Williams, P.W. (2001). The evolving images of wine tourism destinations. *Tourism Recreation Research*, 26(2), 3-10.

The Organization
of Wine Tourism in France:
The Involvement
of the French Public Sector

Jetske van Westering
Emmanuelle Niel

SUMMARY. This paper aims to present the outcome of research into French public sector management of wine tourism, undertaken in 2001. The sample for the research consisted of those working in an executive position within the Comites Departemental or Regional de Tourisme in wine areas. Although smaller wine regions were contacted it was found that only in the big wine regions did this function exist. In addition to the wine regions two other government institutions (Maison de la France and AFIT, l'Association Francaise d'Ingenieurie Touristique) were interviewed for the study, with partial success. The main conclusions of the study are that: insufficient research into data have been collected for the national strategy, especially of wine tourist profiles; the French public sector is composed of many bodies working at different levels–national, regional, local, which, despite having a clear definition to their

Jetske van Westering and Emmanuelle Niel are affiliated with the School of Management, University of Surrey, Guildford, Surrey, UK (E-mail: J.Van-Westering@surrey.ac.uk).

[Haworth co-indexing entry note]: "The Organization of Wine Tourism in France: The Involvement of the French Public Sector." van Westering, Jetske, and Emmanuelle Niel. Co-published simultaneously in *Journal of Travel & Tourism Marketing* (The Haworth Hospitality Press, an imprint of The Haworth Press, Inc.) Vol. 14, No. 3/4, 2003, pp. 35-47; and: *Wine, Food, and Tourism Marketing* (ed: C. Michael Hall) The Haworth Hospitality Press, an imprint of The Haworth Press, Inc., 2003, pp. 35-47. Single or multiple copies of this article are available for a fee from The Haworth Document Delivery Service [1-800-HAWORTH, 9:00 a.m. - 5:00 p.m. (EST). E-mail address: docdelivery@haworthpress.com].

responsibilities and duties seem to have difficulties in working together towards collective goals; research into wine tourism operation and goals was not undertaken with or in all wine regions, draft objectives show priorities of some regions but not others; and communications between involved parties is often slow due to differing political loyalties. *[Article copies available for a fee from The Haworth Document Delivery Service: 1-800-HAWORTH. E-mail address: <docdelivery@haworthpress.com> Website: <http://www.HaworthPress.com> © 2003 by The Haworth Press, Inc. All rights reserved.]*

KEYWORDS. Wine tourism, public sector, France

INTRODUCTION

With 75 million foreign visitors recorded in 2000 and 76.5 million in 2001, France emerges as the world's number one country destination in terms of visitor numbers (Maison de la France 2002, personal communication). This reaffirms that France, with its diversity of tourism products, is an attractive destination.

The profile of France as a holiday destination is undoubtedly augmented by its gastronomy: the reputation of its cuisine is renowned. Each region has a distinct set of specialties that are deeply rooted in culture and with every meal the cultural heritage of the region is digested (van Westering, 2000). It is indeed impossible for visitors to France to escape the role of wine in the meal and the overall importance of wine to French culture. Figures from recent research (Choisy, 1996) emphasize the potential of wine tourism as an emerging tourist attraction for France. Wine tourism is certainly not a new product for France; the main wine regions have long since received visitors. The reputation of wines, such as Bordeaux and Burgundy, attracted wine lovers from both France and abroad to such areas long before the beginning of the Twentieth Century. The main growth in wine tourism however is of a more recent date; Mallon (1996) observed that some wine producers had started to attract visitors to wineries, in order to sell directly to customers, in the 1980s. Today such direct sales represent an important part of the wine trade, particularly in Alsace and Burgundy. Frochot (2000) cites the example of Beaune (Burgundy) where a local wine house, La Reine Pedauque, attracted 130,000 visitors in 1997. The home market is an important market for these direct sales, but with French wine consumption consistently in decline (Productschap voor Gedistilleerde Dranken, 1998) the need to find other markets is imperative. Forecasts from the World Tourism Organization (2000) from before September 11, 2001 indicate that tourism to Europe will double over the next 20 years. It is anticipated that France will retain its pole position, although a reduction in the rise, or a stagnation in the number of visitors from its main continental markets (Germany, Italy and Switzerland) is projected. In order to retain this lead France will need to diversify its products. With its reputation for wines, wine tourism as one such diversification could ensure France sustains its position as the leading destination in Europe to benefit from tourist visits and revenues. Until recently all attempts to attract wine tourists, or to provide for the needs of wine tourists were taken at an individual local level, a level which had little impact, if any, nationally. This may be set to change with fresh initiatives emerging from the public sector. Proposals for the development of a strategy for wine tourism in France are currently under discussion. Clearly such a strategy will have widespread implications for the overall organization and development of wine tourism in France, the latter being the substance of this paper, however, the paper takes on a fuller remit in the investigation of the organization of wine tourism in France. It particularly focuses on:

- the move of the management of wine tourism from the private initiative to the public sector, and the involvement of the French public sector in the organization of its wine tourism,
- determining the current input of the authorities (local, regional, national) in wine tourism in France and the level of co-operation between them,
- identifying the authority/ies responsible for the planning, development and implementation of the proposed strategy for wine tourism,
- the contents of the wine tourism strategy,
- the future role of the public sector in the management of wine tourism in France.

With the above research issues specified, public sector organizations involved in tourism at national, regional and local level were contacted. This move was primarily taken to locate the organizations involved in wine tourism. Seven were identified (two at national level and five at regional level) and invited to take part in this research; five (one at national level and four at regional level) accepted and took part in the interview-based research in 2001.

THE INFRASTRUCTURE OF TOURISM IN FRANCE

The organization of tourism in France presents a somewhat complex picture. This is largely due to the fact that there is no single authority that has exclusive rights or complete jurisdiction over the organization of tourism. A multitude of organizations is active in tourism at the national, regional and local level and, as is often the case when many groups are involved, the interactions between these are difficult to identify, especially when no composite picture is available. Figure 1 sets out to address this omission. As such it presents an overview of the public sector organizations active in tourism.

- The Secretariat d'Etat au Tourisme (SET) is part of the Ministry of Facilities, Transport and Accommodation. It is the highest office responsible for tourism in France being in charge of monitoring, researching and developing tourism. SET has two divisions:

  - the Direction du Tourisme (responsible for the implementation of tourism policies and developing tourism in the country), and
  - the Inspection Generale du Tourisme (responsible for inspecting, auditing and control of tourism).

- The Conseil National du Tourisme (CNT) is under the direction of SET. It equates to a Parliament for tourism. Meeting twice annually, chaired by the minister in charge of tourism, its main aim is to act as a consultative body and to govern the industry.
- La Maison de la France (MDF), a semi-governmental organization, also falls under SET's direction. It is responsible for developing commercial interests in France, and promoting these as a tourist destination for foreign markets. All projects are undertaken with partners from industry (Air France and Galeries Lafayette for example); these partners are also co-funding MDF.
- L'Agence Francaise de l'Ingenieurie Touristique (AFIT) also falls under the auspices of the Ministry. Its main mission is to develop public interest and active partnerships between the public and private sectors in order to encourage the development of an efficient and consistent tourist supply. AFIT's membership comprises nine ministries and thirty-six private or public organizations.
- L'Observatoire National du Tourisme (ONT) is a private company of public interest and is therefore, under French law, entitled to receive subsidies from the French Government as well as donations from other companies. Its main aim is to collect, update and dis-

seminate all economic information about the tourism industry. The ONT issues several publications including the annual report on tourism. It also organizes workshops on a range of topics; the situation in the accommodation sector, the foreign markets, or the state of the economy being examples.

The above delineates the national situation (Swarbrooke, 1992/93). Having stated this, the number of organizations related to tourism is actually much higher, although many of these exist in name only and are inactive.

The regional and departmental situation is equally extensive. For administrative purposes France is divided in 22 regions, which in turn are subdivided into 96 (plus 4 overseas) departments–each with their own administration. Both the regions and the departments have their own tourism offices:

- the Comites Regionaux du Tourisme (CRT) with an average budget of almost FF 19 million,
- the Comites Departementaux du Tourisme (CDT) with approximately FF 7.5 million each,
- the Offices du Tourisme (OT), the Syndicates d'Initiative (SI) or the Service Loisirs-Acceuil pour la destination France (SLA) are the tourist boards and offices which provide local publicity and deal with the day to day affairs regarding tourism. The differences between OT, SI and SLA are mainly found in the way they have been established legally,
- The Federations of CRTs, CDTs, OTs, SIs, and SLAs; each has its own federation,
- the Confederation Nationale du Tourisme in which all these federations are represented.

Having identified the main and semi-public organizations responsible for tourism overall, the research moved to a clarification of the authorities involved with wine tourism. Again the concern here was directed at the national, regional and departmental situation and the cooperation that exists between them.

THE ORGANIZATION OF WINE TOURISM IN FRANCE

At the national level two organizations, la Maison de la France (MDF) and l'Agence Francaise de l'Ingenieurie Touristique (AFIT), have re-

FIGURE 1

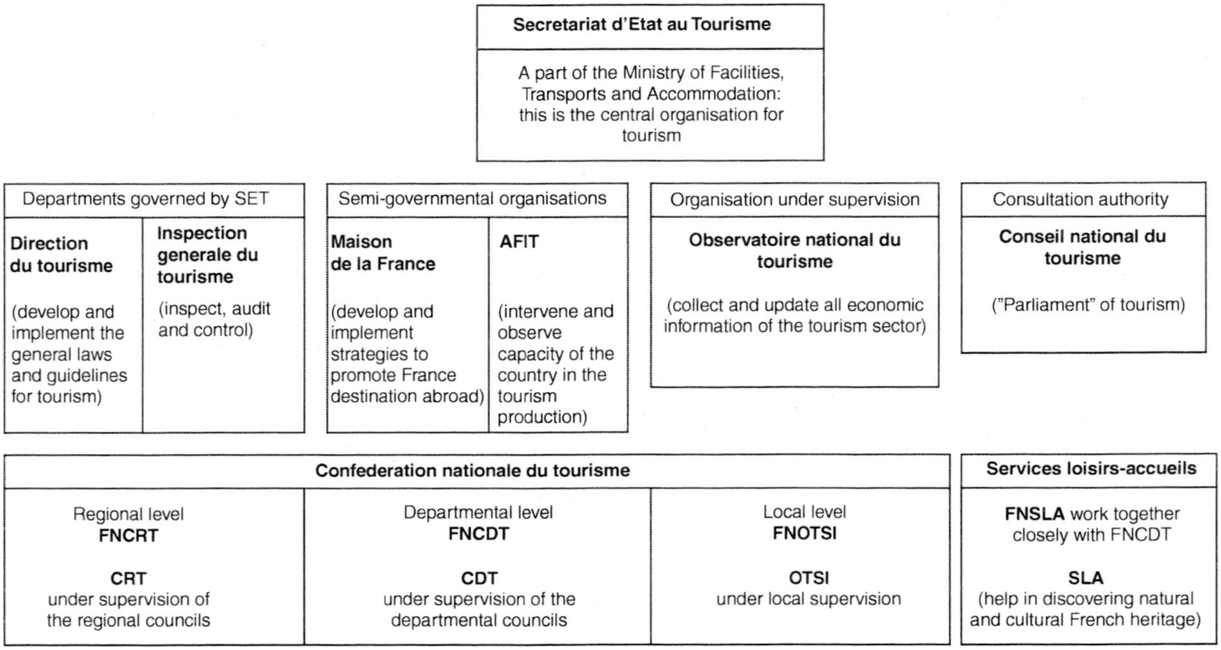

Secretariat d'Etat au Tourisme

A part of the Ministry of Facilities, Transports and Accommodation: this is the central organisation for tourism

Consultation authority
Conseil national du tourisme
("Parliament" of tourism)

Departments governed by SET	
Direction du tourisme	**Inspection generale du tourisme**
(develop and implement the general laws and guidelines for tourism)	(inspect, audit and control)

Semi-governmental organisations	
Maison de la France	**AFIT**
(develop and implement strategies to promote France destination abroad)	(intervene and observe capacity of the country in the tourism production)

Organisation under supervision
Observatoire national du tourisme
(collect and update all economic information of the tourism sector)

Services loisirs-accueils
FNSLA work together closely with FNCDT
SLA (help in discovering natural and cultural French heritage)

Confederation nationale du tourisme		
Regional level **FNCRT**	Departmental level **FNCDT**	Local level **FNOTSI**
CRT under supervision of the regional councils	**CDT** under supervision of the departmental councils	**OTSI** under local supervision

cently been involved in wine tourism and have played a central role in the development of the wine tourism strategy.

At the regional level two situations seem to exist; either the public sector aided by the private sector, or the private sector alone, is in charge. In the five biggest wine regions (Rhone-Alpes, Bourgogne, Alsace, Bordeaux and Champagne) the public sector is involved in wine tourism at either regional level (CRT) or departmental level (CDT), but not both. Practice involves the nomination of someone of high rank, e.g., at director or deputy director level, as having overall responsibility for wine tourism. In the research the respondents from CRTs and CDTs regarded wine tourism as only a part of their work (ranging from considerable to little) and indicated scant co-operation between public sector organizations on the subject of wine tourism. OT's and SLA's involvement lies in the distribution of brochures to tourists and in the sales of wine tours, or packages–they are not involved in the management of wine tourism.

The research revealed that until recently wine tourism in most wine regions was organized by the private sector. Organizations such as the Comites, Conseils or Bureaux Interprofessionnels du Vin (du Bourgogne–CIB, de Champagne–CIC, etc.) are funded by the wine industry in the particular wine region. Originally the Comites Interprofessionel du Vin (CIV) were only involved in issues related to wine production, regulation, export and consumption–today they are also involved in bringing wine producers and potential customers together, their role in tourism in, and to the region has grown. The CIVs are clearly the main bodies in most wine regions involved in wine tourism–respondents from the CDTs and CRTs emphasized this by reporting their reliance on the work of the CIVs. Respondents indicated the lack of evaluation of wine tourism. This was seen to lie in the failure of public sector organizations and many wine professionals (particularly the vignerons) to recognize the existence and importance of wine tourism. Irrespective of the failure at this level, the implementation of a coherent strategy from the national level is now in progress.

THE NATIONAL STRATEGY FOR WINE TOURISM

Plans to develop a national wine tourism strategy resulted from AFIT's research (2000a, 2000b, 2000c) into the demand, as well as the supply, of wine tourism. Despite AFIT's approach to all wine regions only six wine regions (Gironde, Alsace, Cher, Drome, Champagne and the Vallee du Rhone) participated. The outcome of this research was made available to each participating region but not collated into national results. This research, however, formed the basis of MDF's plan to develop a national strategy for wine tourism. MDF's main partner in the development of this strategy is the Societe de promotion de l'agroalimentaire francais (SOPEXA), the semi-governmental controlled company engaged in the promotion of French food products. MDF organized (June 2000) an initial seminar in Beaune, Burgundy; this was by invitation only. The intention of the seminar was to draw up a proposal for the national strategy for wine tourism; agreement for the proposal was to be sought in October 2000. Subsequent to this MDF would present a three-year action plan (to be started in 2002) to be agreed in June 2001. MDF claimed that all partners (AFIT, SOPEXA, all CIV, CDT, CRT and OTSI) had participated; however, this was denied by three of our interviewees. It appears that not all CRTs/CDTs were invited to the seminars as claimed.

These seminars led to the publication of "A strategy for wine tourism" (MDF, 2000). This documents the following rationale for the development of a wine tourism strategy:

- Benefits from wine tourism have been rising considerably over the last few years,
- The main markets for French wine tourism are, in descending order: Germany, the UK, Belgium, the USA and Japan. There is strong development potential in each of these markets,
- There is recognition for the close links between the wine industry and the tourism industry. Recently, professionals from these two industries have started to co-operate, although there is a regional disparity in the commitment shown,
- The AFIT research identified 5,000 cellars, domains or wineries that are open for visits, and
- Nine categories of activities, including wine routes, visits to wineries, tracks and paths through vineyards, tours or stays organized in the vineyard, educational courses about wine, wine musea, "Maisons du Vin"–a more interactive type of museum, wine fetes, festivals and fairs, exhibitions and auctions.

This rationale led to the formulation of a series of objectives. For the tourism industry the objectives are:

- To increase the number of tourists to wine tourism areas.
- To increase tourism turnover.

- To increase direct sales in the wineries.
- To increase the reputation of the wine tourism areas.

For the wine world the objectives are similar:

- To increase sales in wineries and their environment.
- To increase the reputation of the wine area.

The objectives for the two industries are integrated as illustrated in the virtuous circle model (Figure 2). This demonstrates the interrelationship between the wine and tourism industries and the importance of each industry to the other. In addition to the rationale and objectives, stages targeting the main markets with promotional activities (see Figure 3) are proposed.

Other actions include the distribution of a brochure developed to heighten foreign opinion leaders' awareness of the importance of wine tourism; the edition of a French vineyard tourism map, and the creation of Internet pages dedicated to wine tourism.

THE MANAGEMENT OF WINE TOURISM IN THE FUTURE– RESPONDENTS' VIEWS

Interviewees were divided on the issue as to whether or not the wine tourism strategy would bring a better organization of wine tourism: those who had taken part in the seminars organized by the MDF expected the final strategy to specify responsibilities and duties of the CRT's and CDT's. Others did not think that much would change. Respondents agreed that the French tourism public sector is not "too badly" organized and is capable of developing wine tourism, whilst others were concerned about the lack of one central responsible authority.

Also, the willingness of CDT's and CRT's employees to co-operate is in question; they are subordinate to CRT members who are elected for six years but half are re-elected every three years and therefore an issue of political interference is raised. In the Gironde, a subdivision of Aquitaine, the Conseil General on which the CDT depends, and the Conseil Regional to which the CRT is attached, are run currently by two different political parties, each have totally opposing views to the development of tourism–thus adding to the dichotomy. In addition, French networks related to wine tourism are non-existent and European initiatives, such as the European Council of Wine Routes, are viewed with

FIGURE 2. The Virtuous Circle

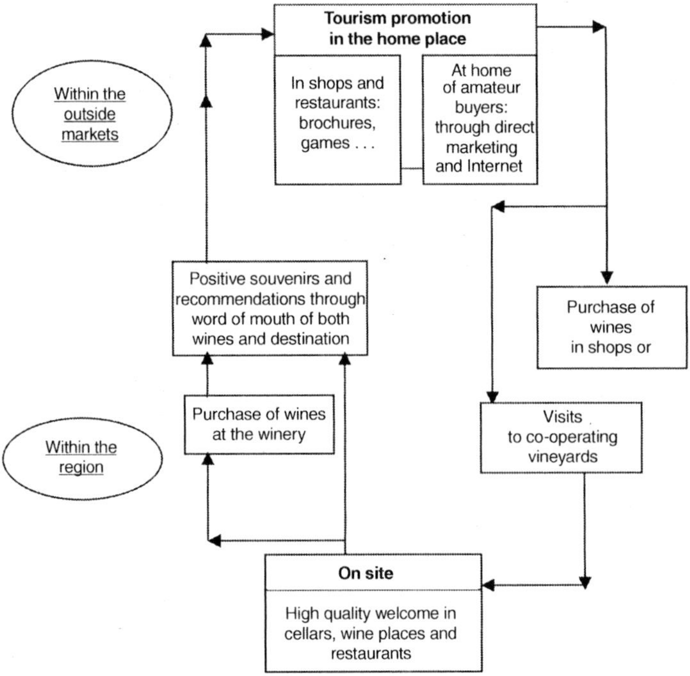

Source: MDF, 2000

suspicion. All respondents agreed that membership of the latter is expected to reap less significant results than the currently proposed sales campaigns in selected markets.

CONCLUSIONS

The French public sector comprises many bodies, all working on tourism but at different levels–national, regional, departmental. Irrespective of a clear definition of their responsibilities and duties, each seems to have difficulty in working together towards collective goals. The development of a national strategy for wine tourism has been initiated by semi-governmental organizations and it is currently unclear whether or not these organizations were selected to undertake the work, and if so by whom, or whether they just selected themselves. From an

FIGURE 3. Steps for Promotional Activities Abroad

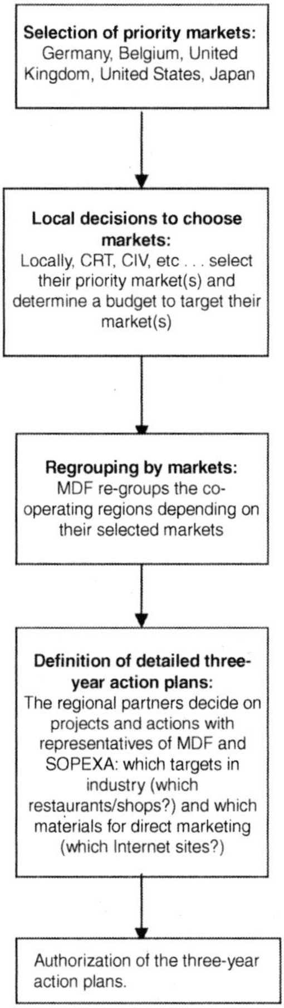

```
┌─────────────────────────────┐
│ Selection of priority markets: │
│ Germany, Belgium, United      │
│ Kingdom, United States, Japan │
└─────────────────────────────┘
              │
              ▼
┌─────────────────────────────┐
│   Local decisions to choose  │
│          markets:            │
│ Locally, CRT, CIV, etc . . . select │
│   their priority market(s) and │
│ determine a budget to target their │
│          market(s)           │
└─────────────────────────────┘
              │
              ▼
┌─────────────────────────────┐
│    Regrouping by markets:    │
│   MDF re-groups the co-      │
│ operating regions depending on │
│   their selected markets     │
└─────────────────────────────┘
              │
              ▼
┌─────────────────────────────┐
│ Definition of detailed three- │
│     year action plans:       │
│ The regional partners decide on │
│    projects and actions with │
│  representatives of MDF and  │
│  SOPEXA: which targets in    │
│      industry (which         │
│ restaurants/shops?) and which │
│ materials for direct marketing │
│   (which Internet sites?)    │
└─────────────────────────────┘
              │
              ▼
┌─────────────────────────────┐
│ Authorization of the three-year │
│        action plans.         │
└─────────────────────────────┘
```

Source: MDF, 2000

analysis of the French tourism structure and respondents' views, it appears that the Direction du Tourisme would be the most appropriate institution for undertaking the development of strategies, not the current MDF/SOPEXA combination. The research revealed that only one person is working on the national wine tourism strategy for MDF. It seems an almost impossible task for one person to collect and analyze all the data on which a coherent national strategy is to be developed.

Arguably it may be better to have a strategy for wine tourism than no strategy at all. If in future the existing strategy is to be evaluated (and this is not indicated) the following recommendations might be taken into consideration:

- The AFIT research into wine tourism operations was not undertaken in cooperation with or in all wine regions, nor were the subsequent goals, set during the seminars and forming the basis of the draft wine tourism strategy, agreed in cooperation with or in all wine regions. Thus the priorities of some regions were left unaccounted.
- No data were collected regarding wine tourist profiles in the AFIT research neither were profiles of wine tourists taken into account in the wine tourism strategy. The collection of standardized data, related to both demand and supply, might be recommended if consistency is to be achieved.
- Strategies need regular updating. More resources (human) must be made available at all levels–CRT/CDT as well as MDF–to cope with the pressures of collecting appropriate data, as well as planning, motivating, operating and controlling actions related to wine tourism.
- The evaluation and control phase of the strategy has been insufficiently considered. The Observatoire National du Tourisme should be involved in the analysis of data as well as in the format and type of data to be collected. Monitoring and control functions could be put in place by the Direction du Tourisme to measure the effectiveness of actions undertaken.
- Interactions between the public sector organizations involved in wine tourism are often absent due to decentralization, different sources of funding and the lack of interdependence. Communication between involved parties needs to be improved. Currently this is often slow due to differing political loyalties. Workshops and conferences could help to allow rapport to be built and national networks to be established.

France has the advantage over many other European countries where as yet wine tourism is underdeveloped. Spain and Italy offer similar activities in their wine regions but have also only recently started to structure and manage their wine tourism products. If France is to retain its competitive edge and capitalize on its strategic assets it will need to establish basic management processes in its wine tourism sector. The need for a strategic plan and infrastructure is recognized by those involved in wine and wine tourism. The route to its achievement, however, is fraught with problems: until these are fully addressed it is unlikely that a coherent strategy can be established. Despite this, the efforts of both the wine and tourism industries need to be applauded.

REFERENCES

Agence Francaise de l'Ingenierie Touristique (2000a). *Etude sur le Tourism Viti-Vinicole en Gironde: Note de synthese*. Agence Francaise de l'Ingenierie Touristique.

Agence Francaise de l'Ingenierie Touristique (2000b). *Etude sur le Tourism Viti-Vinicole en Champagne: Note de synthese*. Agence Francaise de l'Ingenierie Touristique.

Agence Francaise de l'Ingenierie Touristique (2000c). *Etude sur le Tourism Viti-Vinicole en Haute-Alsace: Note de synthese*. Agence Francaise de l'Ingenierie Touristique.

Choisy, C. (1996). Le poids du tourisme viti-vinicole, *Espaces*, 140, 31-33.

Frochot, I. (2000). Wine tourism in France: A paradox? In Hall, C.M., Sharples, L., Cambourne, B. and Macionis, N. (ed.) *Wine Tourism around the World*, Oxford: Butterworth-Heinemann, 67-80.

Maison de la France (2000). *Une Strategie pour la Tourisme Viti-Vinicole*, unpublished document, Maison de la France.

Mallon, P. (1996). Vin et tourisme: Un developpement dans la diversite. *Espaces*, 140, 75-81.

Productschap voor Gedistilleerde Dranken (1998). *World Drink Trends*, Henley-on-Thames: NTC Publications.

Swarbrooke, J. (1992/1993). Public sector policy in tourism: A comparative study of France and Britain. *Insights*, 5, 33-46.

Van Westering, J. (1999). Heritage and gastronomy: the pursuits of the 'new tourist.' *International Journal of Heritage Studies*, 5(2), 75-81.

World Tourism Organization (2000). *Tourism Market Trends 2000*, www.world-tourism.org.

Cider and the Marketing of the Tourism Experience in Somerset, England: Three Case Studies

Ann Elizabeth Sharples

SUMMARY. The paper provides a background to the history, development and importance of the cider industry to the county. A case study approach is then adopted, in order to demonstrate the richness of cider experiences available to the tourist travelling both through, and within, Somerset. Three case studies of individual firms are provided. The paper notes that a firm's reasons for engaging in tourism bear great similarities to those utilized by wineries. The paper also highlights the importance of collective marketing strategies at both the firm and business level. *[Article copies available for a fee from The Haworth Document Delivery Service: 1-800-HAWORTH. E-mail address: <docdelivery@haworthpress.com> Website: <http://www.HaworthPress.com> © 2003 by The Haworth Press, Inc. All rights reserved.]*

KEYWORDS. Cider tourism, destination marketing, Somerset

Ann Elizabeth Sharples is Senior Lecturer, School of Sport & Leisure Management, Sheffield Hallam University, City Campus, Sheffield S1 1WB UK (E-mail: l.A.sharples@shu.ac.uk).

The author wishes to thank Julian Temperley, Louisa Sheppy, Margie Perry and James Crowden for their help with this article.

[Haworth co-indexing entry note]: "Cider and the Marketing of the Tourism Experience in Somerset, England: Three Case Studies." Sharples, Ann Elizabeth. Co-published simultaneously in *Journal of Travel & Tourism Marketing* (The Haworth Hospitality Press, an imprint of The Haworth Press, Inc.) Vol. 14, No. 3/4, 2003, pp. 49-60; and: *Wine, Food, and Tourism Marketing* (ed: C. Michael Hall) The Haworth Hospitality Press, an imprint of The Haworth Press, Inc., 2003, pp. 49-60. Single or multiple copies of this article are available for a fee from The Haworth Document Delivery Service [1-800-HAWORTH, 9:00 a.m. - 5:00 p.m. (EST). E-mail address: docdelivery@haworthpress.com].

10.1300/J073v14n03_03

INTRODUCTION:
CIDER, APPLES AND THE SOMERSET LANDSCAPE

The connections between apples, cider and the landscape of Somerset run deep and is a core part of the county's image (Copas 2001). Folklore would argue that apples, like vines, were introduced to Britain by the Romans during the time of Ceasar in 55 BC. Apples, unlike vines however, are indigenous to Britain and wild crab apples have been part of the Somerset landscape for many years previous to the Roman occupation. For example, the town of Glastonbury in the Northern part of Somerset was also called Avallon or Ynys Avallac, The Isle of Apples by the Iron Age tribes who lived there (Copas 2001), an indicator that apples have been an important part of this region for many centuries.

There are many early references to the production of cider in this county, many linked to monasteries in the area. Monks were keen gardeners and there is much evidence to suggest that they were skilled in the art of cider making. For example, In 1230 there is the first listing of cider presses as a source of income in a Royal Charter granted to Jocelin, Bishop of Bath, and in 1536 at the dissolution of the monasteries, many orchards, cider presses and stills came onto the open market (Crowden 2001). Since these early beginnings the cider industry in Somerset has experienced its good times and bad. Crowden (1999) describes the late Seventeenth Century and early Eighteenth Century as being the "heyday" for cider production in the UK and it was certainly during this time that great advances were made in improving fermentation techniques, yeast usage, the selection of apple varieties to suit particular soil and climatic conditions, and the management of orchards. Unfortunately, by the end of the nineteenth century the market for cider was in decline, being squeezed by "wine from above and beer from below" (Crowden 1999) and its reputation was also suffering. The future for cider making looked bleak but the input of enthusiasts such as Sir Robert Neville Grenville helped to rescue a flagging industry (Copas 2001). Cider apple varieties were collected, experimental orchards were set up and small cider factories opened which in turn led to the creation of larger corporations; for example, Bulmers, Taunton Cider, Coates and Gaymers (Crowden 1999).

Over this last century, there has been some loss of traditional orchards in Somerset as farmers and landowners have ripped out trees in favor of more profitable crops; but the tables are now being turned, and in 1987 Somerset County Council became the first council to introduce a scheme for grant aided replanting of traditional orchards (Crowden,

2001). Organizations such as Common Ground (*www.commonground. org.uk* 2002) are also helping the fight to protect and preserve orchards, and the range of apple varieties that grow there. Currently, the larger manufacturers offer a range of internationally recognised brands available in all of the major supermarkets, including a range of "designer ciders" aimed to meet the needs of a younger teenage cider market. Due to their "mass" production techniques they are not particularly accessible to the visitor market. In contrast, we are witnessing an exciting renaissance (Copas 2001) in the cider world through the development of new products that have sparked interest, renewed confidence, and provided a powerful vehicle for the promotion of Somerset as one of the most significant cider producing regions in the world.

Cider, like many other drink products, has had its "rises and falls" with regards to its popularity and markets over the years but presently is enjoying a modest revival within the UK, with cider making having doubled in production in the last 20 years (National Association of Cider Makers (NACM) 2000). Information regarding the true size and nature of the total cider UK, market is not easily accessible however. The NACM (2000), who produce approximately 90% of the UK's cider, reported that in the year 2000, over 600 million litres of cider were produced within the UK making it the largest producer in Europe. However, this figure does not include information derived from the many smaller scale cider makers who operate within the South West and who sell much of their cider locally or from the farm gate (Bunker 1999). Over the last decade, there has been a gradual decline in the sales of traditional farm-house cider (Temperley 2001) but there has been a growing interest in the production of specialist ciders, such as sparkling cider, single variety ciders (ciders produced from one variety of apple) and Cider Brandy. One example of this change of direction was seen in 1989 when The Somerset Brandy Company, situated in Kingsbury Episcopi, was granted, by HM customs, the first full cider distilling license in recorded history (The Somerset Cider Brandy Co. Ltd. & Burrow Hill Cider 2001). This paved the way for the setting up of several cider distilleries within other areas of the UK.

Cider production has always been viewed as a good tourist "spectator" activity and there are few more evocative scenes than watching, and smelling, the pressing of apples in the Autumn at a farmyard during cider-making season. Allowing tourists to watch this activity is an opportunity for cider makers to "showcase" their expertise and share information before giving visitors a chance to sample and purchase cider. This interest has been fuelled by demands for more "genuine" or "original" products amongst some consumers (Ritzer 1996), and Somerset cider, made in the traditional way, is just that. Apples are gathered from local orchards before being washed and pressed, the juice then being transferred to wooden casks where a natural fermentation takes place without the use of any additives. This is now a good selling point for many cider producers, many making the point by allowing visitors to walk through their orchards and "touch" the apples in order to promote the closeness between raw material on the trees and the finished product in the bottle. The business developments at the local level have been matched by initiatives at the governmental level to improve rural industries, such as food and tourism, following the foot and mouth crisis.

Since 2000 there has been an emergence of several initiatives that link food, tourism, and the countryside (McCarthy 2002); for example, The Countryside Agency's "Eat the View" campaign, aimed at promoting sustainable local products (*www.eat-the-view.org.uk*). Also, the launch of the "Food and Drink in Tourism" scheme, a major new project with funding from the English Tourism Council with an aim to develop the local distinctiveness of certain regions through its food and drink culture (*www.visitheartofengland.com*). Still, at the pilot stage, it is envisaged that this project will be rolled out around the country within the next two years. A joint publication between the Countryside Agency and the English Tourism Council (English Tourism Council 2001) includes recommendations about the use of local produce and gastronomy as a vehicle for enriching the rural tourism experience. However, despite the development of cider tourism there is little attention given to this drink in comparison to that given to wine (e.g., Hall and Mitchell 2001), even though the product is an essential part of the food tourism experience in many parts of the world, and Somerset in particular. Therefore, this article presents case studies of three cider businesses in Somerset to highlight their involvement in tourism and their contribution to regional marketing. All case studies were written following field work in the area and interviews with the businesses concerned.

THE SOMERSET CIDER BRANDY COMPANY LTD. AND BURROW HILL CIDER

This cider works is situated at Burrow Hill in the village of Kingsbury Episcopi where the director, Julian Temperley, manages 130 acres of traditional orchards containing over 40 varieties of apples. This is currently the largest traditional orchard in Somerset. Temperley is the innovator of the Somerset cider industry and has managed to become one of the agricultural success stories of the region as he has steered his company to explore new products, and hence new markets, over recent years. Despite an enormous respect for tradition and traditional cider making techniques Temperley rightly identified that the farmhouse cider market was in decline and in attempt to secure his business has recently moved into the production of Cider Brandy. He sees distilling as his future. Temperley still produces a traditional cider, Burrow Hill, pressed from a range of locally grown cider apples, and fermented in oak barrels, which he sells by draught from the barrel or by the bottle. This cider is sold to a number of pubs in the area.

The company also produces two single variety ciders using Stoke Red and Kingston Black apples. Both these are specialist dry, sparkling ciders made using "Methode Champenoise" which have won great support from wine critics (Somerset Cider Brandy Co. Ltd. & Burrow Hill Cider 2001). Two varieties of apple juice are also sold at the cider works and Temperley has recently acquired more land to enable him to grow more Cox, Russet and Bramley apples to support this aspect of his production. The granting of a full cider distilling license, in 1989, however, allowed Temperley to specialise on the making of a premium product which has earned him recognition as a master in his field. He now produces a range of excellent Cider Brandies including a three year old product, aptly named Somerset Royal, and superb five year and ten year old brandies. He also produces an Apple Eau de Vie (Apple spirit) and the very popular "Kingston Black." This is a combination of Cider Brandy with Kingston Black apple juice blended to create an 18% Apple aperitif. All of the Cider Brandy products have received excellent reviews from critics (*www.ciderbrandy.co.uk* 2002). The elegant bottle and label designs used for the Cider Brandy range and in particular the Kingston Black product are a strong statement that Cider is no longer a simple country drink. These are bottles fit to grace any dinner table, and Temperley has successfully persuaded many of the UK top food shops, including Fortnum & Mason, Lea & Sandeman, Sally Clarke, Provender and the Chatsworth Farm Shop to stock his products.

The visitor to Burrow Hill will not be greeted by a large car park, a well organized visitor centre explaining the rudiments of cider making or a shop selling local crafts and gifts. The yard at Burrow hill may look a little unkempt, at first glance, but, for the visitor who is willing to look beyond this, there is the opportunity to see "authentic" cider making operations. Temperley gives visitors the chance to view his impressive cider stills, housed securely behind plated glass, experience the orchards either by following a trail or from a "viewing room," at the top of a specially constructed barn, and possibly glimpse the cellars where the sparkling ciders are racked. There is also the added joy of sampling some of the best ciders and cider brandies available within the UK and of watching the maverick of the cider world at work.

R.J. SHEPPY & SON–
A FAMILY BUSINESS

Established in the 1920s, cider making has been an important part of the family since the early 1800s (*www.sheppyscider.co.uk* 2002). Situated in the Vale of Taunton, at Bradford Tone, just a few miles west of Taunton town centre, the Sheppy family manage a farm of over 350 acres, 47 of which are devoted to cider apples. A range of 25-30 apple varieties are grown including the traditional favorites of Kingston Black, Yarlington Mill, Dabinett, Stoke Red, and Tremlett's Bitter. A number of local pubs and shops are supplied but "cellar door" sales are a crucial part of their business.

The range and style of ciders produced has grown and developed over recent years in an attempt to keep pace with a changing cider market. A traditional draught farmhouse cider is still a "mainstay" product in the Sheppys range, as is their "Oakwood" draught premium cider, which has been matured in fine oak vats. These ciders showcase the family's roots and skills in producing and selling cider in the traditional way and give the visitor a chance to sample a style of cider that is unavailable on supermarket shelves and has changed little for many hundreds of years. A comprehensive range of bottled cider is also produced at the cider works, however, including several specialist sparkling ciders, Oakwood Special, Bullfinch and Goldfinch and an award winning strong still cider made from a carefully blended selection of cider apples.

Single variety ciders, available in smaller 500ml bottles, appear to be one of Sheppy's strategies for securing a sound future, however. Their range of Kingston Black, Dabinett, Taylors Gold and Tremletts Bitter packaged in clear bottles and sporting simple, almost minimalist, labels make a definite statement on the shelves of the ciderworks shop. Their clear, fragrant, refreshing nature form a clever contrast to the heavier, more substantial, farmhouse ciders making them ideal food companions and echoing the move in the wine industry for simpler packaging. The recent appearance of Sheppy's cider on several of the major U.K.

super-markets shelves maybe suggests that this is a company not content to live entirely on its traditions. Its' roots maybe firmly planted in Somerset but it has a keen eye on protecting its future as a main player in the UK cider scene. Apple juice has also become an increasingly popular product in their range, possibly reflecting people's desire to consume more healthily, but also providing customers with an opportunity to purchase a "children friendly" product.

Tourists are an important part of the Sheppy's overall philosophy and business plan. The cider works offers the visitor several different "experiences" during their stay including the chance to watch a video which illustrates the cider making process and an opportunity to visit to their "rural life" museum, which houses an interesting collection of agricultural and cider making equipment. Sheppys are also ideally suited to cope with the group visit. Being close to Taunton on a fairly major road and having the advantage of a large car park adjacent to the cider works, it is not surprising that this type of activity is a key part of their offering. Louisa Sheppy reports, however (Sheppy 2002), that this type of business is unfortunately in decline as less people appear to join "interest" groups and churches these days preferring a more individual approach to leisure.

The cider-works and the shop open throughout the year, which Sheppy maintains (Sheppy 2002) is essential despite the fact that the winter months can be slow. The concept of being able to offer products to the local market (especially repeat business) and to the visitor travelling out of season is key. The shop offers cider sampling but also sells a limited range of locally produced food products, books and gifts. A licensed tearoom is also available during the summer months and on bank holidays, whilst a picnic area, a play area and a nature walk ensures that the cider visit has appeal for the "family" market. Sheppy comments (Sheppy 2002) in fact that she sees children as playing an important part in the cider-works future, in particular, the possibility of acquainting and educating school children about rural life.

PERRYS CIDER MILLS–
A TRADITIONAL PRODUCER

This is a cider works proud of its traditions and heritage and keen to preserve the skills of cider making that have been learnt and honed by their family for over 80 years. Perrys is situated in the picturesque village of Dowlish Wake, tucked away in a peaceful valley close to the market town of Ilminster. Despite its "out of the way" location it attracts

a steady stream of visitors throughout the year due to a sensible marketing policy that has kept the business "visible" for many years. Perry's
acreage devoted to cider apples is smaller than Sheppys or the Cider
Brandy company, being in the region of 20 acres, but Perrys is well located to "buy in" apples from other local orchards in order to hit their
annual production levels. They are also keen to stress that they are not
interested in extending their production levels to an unmanageable
level, preferring to stick to well tried and tested methods (Perry 2002).
This is a company which understands the vagaries of the cider market
well, and are therefore content to keep within their limitations, concen-
trating on quality rather than quantity. The idea of "scaling up" to compete for shelf space on the supermarket shelf does not appear to be an
attractive option (Perry 2002).

Perrys produce a range of excellent draught traditional farmhouse
ciders available as medium sweet, medium dry and dry and also a
range of vintage, slightly sparkling, sweet, medium and dry bottled ciders. Single variety ciders are becoming more popular and Perrys offer several, including one made from Morgan Sweet and another
award winner made from Redsteak apples (*http://www.perryscider.co.
uk* 2002). Perrys cider stays "local" serving a few local pubs, but also
selling out of off-licenses and shops in the vicinity and also at the coast,
an ideal market during the summer months. The decline of the cider pub
trade, since the 1960s, has also forced Perrys to reevaluate its business
activity and the family has made a deliberate attempt in recent years to
capture the local "holiday trade" (Perry 2002). The development of the
Cider mill into an attractive and well organized visitor centre for tourists staying in and travelling through the area has been a positive move
in this direction.

For visitors fortunate enough to visit during the Autumn months
there is the opportunity of standing in a sixteenth century barn to wit-
ness the very evocative scene of cider being pressed in the traditional
way. For visitors who arrive at other times of the year they can experience the process via a video or a photographic display. A new barn
houses Perrys museum, an extensive collection of old farm implements,
cider making equipment and farm wagons. There is also a fascinating
display of photos illustrating farming and village life at the turn of the
century. Both individuals and coach parties are well catered for. Their
well stocked shop provides an opportunity to sample and buy their own
range of ciders and apple juices but also demonstrates their commitment to other local producers by stocking a range of locally made foods
and gifts, including Cider Brandy from the Somerset Brandy Company.

CONCLUSION

The three case studies which are provided illustrates the way in which individual cider producers have utilized tourism as a means of establishing a closer relationship with their customers and of maintaining, or even growing, their sales base. The rationale behind such business strategies are extremely similar to that associated with wineries through their cellar-door sales (Hall et al. 2000; Hall and Mitchell 2001), in that tourism provides cider producers with:

- *Increased Consumer Exposure* to product and increased opportunities to sample product.
- *Brand Awareness and Loyalty* through links between producer and consumer, and purchase of branded merchandise.
- *Relationships with Customers.* The opportunity to meet staff and to see "behind the scenes" can lead to positive relationships with consumers which may lead to both direct sales and indirect sales through positive "word of mouth" advertising.
- *Increased Margins* through direct sale to consumer, where the absence of distributor costs is not carried over entirely to the consumer.
- An *Additional Sales Outlet,* or for smaller cider producers who cannot guarantee volume or constancy of supply, the only feasible sales outlet.
- *Marketing Intelligence on Products.* Cider producers can gain instant and valuable feedback on the consumer reaction to their existing products, and are able to trial new additions to their product range.
- *Marketing Intelligence on Customers.* Visits can provide information about consumers.
- *Educational Opportunities.* Visits to producers help create awareness and appreciation of cider, apples and the cider industry, the knowledge and interest generated by this can be expected to result in increased consumption. It is especially interesting to note firms also seeking to educate children at an early age regarding apple and cider production.

In addition, the three firms have all engaged in cooperative behavior with respect to marketing and planning at a regional level while continuing to market themselves separately through the display of "in-house" publicity leaflets in tourist information centres, travel centres, and shops throughout Somerset. Examples of cooperative tourism marketing include their participation in a cider trail launched, appropriately, on

Apple Day, October 21st 2001, which links together 28 cider producers and five apple juice producers in the region as well as providing interesting information about the history of cider, its manufacture, apple varieties and other sources of information (Crowden 2001; Somerset Tourist Department 2002). Indeed, Apple Day itself is an event recently started in the UK by an organization called Common Ground, with the aim to preserve the many hundreds of species of apple that have been traditionally grown in orchards in Britain (*www.commonground. org.uk* 2001).

Significantly the three firms not only promote themselves through food and drink marketing literature in the SouthWest and Somerset. For example, the "All in Good Taste" brochure (South Somerset District Council 2001) and The "Taste of the West" literature and web-site (*http://www.tasteofhtewest.co.uk* 2001). But, most significantly of all, they promote their cider works as being an "attraction" for visitors rather than just being a cider producer through their inclusion on brochures such as "What to do and see in Somerset" (Somerset District Council 2001) and through the "attraction" section on the Somerset Tourism Office web-site (*http://www.somerset.gov.uk/tourism* 2002).

The three firms used as case studies in this article therefore illustrate the integration of cider into tourism marketing at both the level of the firm and the region as well as focusing on promoting themselves as attractions rather than just cider producers. Although cider is the core of their business, they recognize that in order to maintain and grow the market new consumers need to be attracted. Tourism is therefore an essential component of their business strategy in a manner very similar to that recognized elsewhere with respect to wine and food tourism (Hall and Mitchell 2001; Hall et al. 2003).

However, the collective and individual activities of the firms also contribute to the strengthening of both a drinks brand (cider) and a regional brand (Somerset). The successful marketing of any destination is dependent on a range of interrelated factors but includes the identification of the unique selling features of that region, and the selection of an appropriate marketing strategy in order to capture the chosen target market. This article has demonstrated that the realisation of a food or drink product that has an unmistakable link to a geographical area can be a powerful tool for both individual businesses and the region as a whole. This concept is supported by an number of studies which note that regional imagery (Henchion and McIntyre 2000; Hall et al. 2000) plays an important contribution to the niche marketing of food products in rural economies enabling them to differentiate themselves from the homogeneity of standardized products available elsewhere in the marketplace. The "image" of the apple and cider needs no introduction to Somerset. It is an image that has always been there and probably always will, and as such is the perfect marketing tool for tourism to the county as well as that of individual firms. It is hoped that the introduction of the new marketing initiatives in Somerset will keep the miracle of cider alive for both locals and visitors alike and secure a sound future for the region's cider industry.

REFERENCES

Bunker, B. (1999). *Farmhouse Cider and Scrumpy*, Launceston: Bossiney Books.

Copas, L. (2002). *A Somerset Pomona. The Cider Apples of Somerset*, Dorset: The Dovecote Press.

Crowden, J. (1999). *Cider–The Forgotten Miracle*, Cyder Press 2, Somerset.

Crowden, J. (2000). 'Bottling it up' Bristol University magazine, October 2000, Vol. 11, No. 1.

Crowden, J. (2001). *Somerset Cider & Apple Juice, A Guide to Orchards and Cider Makers*. J. Crowden & Somerset County Council.

English Tourism Council (2001). *Working for the Countryside. A strategy for rural tourism in England 2001-2005*. English Tourism Council, London.

Hall, C.M. and Mitchell, R. (2001). Wine and food tourism. In *Special Interest Tourism*, eds. N. Douglas, N. Douglas and R. Derrett, Brisbane: John Wiley & Sons, 307-329.

Hall, C.M., Sharples, L., Mitchell, R., Cambourne, B. & Macionis, N. (Eds.) (2002). *Food Tourism Around the World*. Oxford: Butterworth-Heinemann.

Hall, C.M., Sharples, E., Cambourne, B. & Macionis, N. (Eds.) (2000). *Wine Tourism Around the World: Development, Management and Markets*, Oxford: Butterworth-Heinemann.

Henchion, M. and McIntyre, B. (2000). 'Regional Imagery and quality products: the Irish experience' in *British Food Journal*, Vol. 102 No. 8 p. 630-644.

http://www.eat-the-view.org.uk visited 19.3.2002.

http://www.visitheartofengland.com visited February 2002.

http://www.perryscider.co.uk visited March 2002.

http://www.commonground.org.uk visited March 2002.

http://www.ciderbrandy.co.uk visited March 2002.

McCarthy, M. (2002). 'Make local food focus of rural life' say experts. *The Independent*, 25 January 2002 p.11.

National Association of Cider Makers (NACM). *http://www.cideruk.com* visited October 2001.

Perry, M. (2002). Personal interview conducted March 2002.

Ritzer G. (1996). *McDonaldization of society: An investigation into the changing character of contemporary social life*. Pine Forge Press, California.

Sheppy, L. (2002). Personal interview conducted March 2002.

South Somerset District Council (2001). All in Good Taste brochure, Tourism & Cultural Services, South Somerset District Council, Yeovil.

Somerset Tourism Department (2002). *http://www.somerset.gov.uk/tourism* visited March 2002.

Taste of the West (2001). *http://www.tasteofthewest.co.uk* visited October 2001.

Temperley, J. (2001). Personal Interview conducted October 2001.

The Somerset Cider Brandy Co. Ltd. & Burrow Hill Cider (2001). Publicity leaflet.

Positioning an Emerging Wine Route in the Niagara Region: Understanding the Wine Tourism Market and Its Implications for Marketing

Atsuko Hashimoto
David J. Telfer

SUMMARY. The Niagara Region is not only home to Niagara Falls but also home to an emerging wine route with more than 50 wineries. The Niagara Wine Route has two distinct clusters. The wineries in the east are in the tourist town of Niagara-on-the-Lake, which receives many international visitors while the wineries in the west are not typically on a tourist route and receive more domestic tourists. Through the results of a visitor survey at eight wineries, the paper will illustrate the different markets visiting the Niagara Wine Route and suggests possible implications for marketing strategies for this emerging wine route. *[Article copies available for a fee from The Haworth Document Delivery Service: 1-800-HAWORTH. E-mail address: <docdelivery@haworthpress.com> Website: <http://www.HaworthPress.com> © 2003 by The Haworth Press, Inc. All rights reserved.]*

Atsuko Hashimoto and David J. Telfer are affiliated with the Department of Recreation and Leisure Studies, Brock University, Ontario, Canada.

Address correspondence to: David J. Telfer, Department of Recreation and Leisure Studies, Brock University, St. Catharines, Ontario, Canada L2S 3A1 (E-mail: David. Telfer@Brocku.ca).

[Haworth co-indexing entry note]: "Positioning an Emerging Wine Route in the Niagara Region: Understanding the Wine Tourism Market and Its Implications for Marketing." Hashimoto, Atsuko, and David J. Telfer. Co-published simultaneously in *Journal of Travel & Tourism Marketing* (The Haworth Hospitality Press, an imprint of The Haworth Press, Inc.) Vol. 14, No. 3/4, 2003, pp. 61-76; and: *Wine, Food, and Tourism Marketing* (ed: C. Michael Hall) The Haworth Hospitality Press, an imprint of The Haworth Press, Inc., 2003, pp. 61-76. Single or multiple copies of this article are available for a fee from The Haworth Document Delivery Service [1-800-HAWORTH, 9:00 a.m. - 5:00 p.m. (EST). E-mail address: docdelivery@haworthpress. com].

KEYWORDS. Niagara, wine tourism, marketing, visitor survey

INTRODUCTION

Efforts are underway to diversify the image of the Niagara Region beyond the Falls to incorporate a wine route and position Niagara as a wine and food tourism destination. This paper will examine the changing image of the Niagara Region in the context of the results of a survey to 406 visitors at 8 wineries. More than 50 wineries located in two main clusters in the Niagara Region are working together to help promote the Region (Telfer, 2001a, 2000a, b). In order for its economic survival, as Kotler, Haider and Rein (1993) point out, a destination has to compete with other destinations and regions. It is important for regions to understand their customer base in order to be competitive (Swarbrooke & Horner, 1999; Kotler et al., 1999; Middleton, 1994). In the context of wine tourism, Mitchell and Hall (2001) have also argued that there is a need for a deeper understanding of wine tourists and their behavior. The Niagara Wine Route has two distinct clusters (Telfer, 2001b). The wineries in the eastern section are within the tourist town of Niagara-on-the-Lake and they receive more international visitors. Niagara-on-the-Lake is often on the itinerary after a visit to Niagara Falls. Understanding the international market has proven vital for some of the wineries in Niagara-on-the-Lake. They have successfully identified the Japanese as a segment to market Icewine to as they are required to take back expensive gifts to their friends and relatives (Hashimoto & Telfer, 1999; Telfer & Hashimoto, 2000). The wineries in the west are more difficult to get to and are not typically on a tourist route, hence they receive more domestic tourists. Through the results of the visitor survey, the paper will illustrate the different markets visiting the Niagara Wine Route and suggest possible implications for marketing strategies. These results will be linked to the changing image of the Niagara Region as the focus continues to diversify to attract more visitors.

WINE TOURISM AND MARKETING

Until recently, there has been "relatively little systematic study of the development of wine tourism, the manner in which it is managed and marketed and the people who visit wine regions and experience the wine tourism product" (Cambourne, Macionis & Hall, 2000, p. 320). In an analysis of the literature, Hall et al. (2000) list the advantages of wine tourism for wineries as: increased consumer exposure to products, brand awareness and loyalty, increased margins, additional sales outlet, marketing intelligence on products and consumers, and educational opportunities. The disadvantages include increased costs and management time, capital required and inability to substantially increase sales. The increased recognition of the role of wine tourism is reflected in the need to increase cellar door sales for many wineries. This is especially true in the province of Ontario in Canada where the sale of liquor is very strictly regulated and Ontario wineries rely heavily on cellar door sales.

Wine tourism has been defined as the "visitation to vineyards, wineries, wine festivals and wine shows for which grape wine tasting and/or experiencing the attributes of a grape wine region are the prime motivating factors for visitors" (Hall, 1996; Macionis, 1996). Peters (1997) also links the concept of wine tourism to the land and suggests that when viticulture is successful, it transforms the local landscape into a combination of agriculture, industry and tourism. Peters (1997) refers to wine regions as "winescapes." Hall (2002) argues that wine, food and tourism industries rely on regional branding for market leverage and promotion and thus the appellation, or the regional "brands" become an important source of differentiation and value added for rural regions. The importance of geographic location will become apparent in the case of this study, as there are two identifiable clusters of wineries in the Niagara Region, which can be promoted as such.

While it is recognised that the region plays an important point in marketing, recently has there been a shift towards understanding the consumer behavior of wine tourists (Mitchell, Hall & McIntosh, 2000; Mitchell and Hall 2001). In an analysis of pervious studies, it is suggested that a wine tourist is usually 30-50 years of age, in the moderate to high-income bracket and comes from within or in close proximity to the wine region (Mitchell, Hall & McIntosh 2000). However, as pointed out by Mitchell, Hall and McIntosh (2000, p. 123), "profiles of wine tourists in one region should not automatically be assumed to be the same as in another, or even from one winery to another." Understanding the differences between winery visitors becomes very important for marketers and winery operators in targeting potential visitors (Mitchell, Hall & McIntosh, 2000). This paper seeks to examine the differences between visitors to the wineries in the Niagara Region and to suggest potential marketing strategies for these different types of visitors. Before examining the results of this study, the paper turns to a brief overview of the changes in the wine industry that have led to the development of wine tourism in Niagara.

CHANGES IN THE WINE INDUSTRY IN NIAGARA

The wine industry has undergone a tremendous amount of change in the Niagara Region since the mid-1970s. There have been three main factors, which have attributed to the transformation in the industry. These changes will be highlighted briefly here; however, readers are directed to Telfer (2000 a, b, 2001a, b) for more detailed historical accounts. The first major change occurred in 1975 when Inniskillin Winery was granted the first estate winery license in Ontario since prohibition. They led an industry shift towards premium wine production using *vitis vinifera* grape varieties and soon, other estate wineries such as Chateau des Charmes, Hillebrand Estates, Cave Spring Cellars, and Henry of Pelham Family Estates Winery began opening (www.wineroute.com/Ifacts.html). The second major factor was the introduction of the Free Trade Agreement with the United States and a ruling by the General Agreement on Tariffs and Trade (GATT), eliminating the preferential treatment for Ontario wines. The result was the introduction of the Grape Acreage Reduction Program (GARP) negotiated by the Federal and Provincial governments leading to the removal up to 3,300 ha of grapes, mostly the inferior *vitis labrusca* and *vitis riparia* varieties. Much of the new planing was of the *vitis vinifera* varieties (Chapman, 1994). The third major factor was the introduction of the Vintners Quality Alliance (VQA) in 1988, which set new standards for the quality of wine. The use of VQA on a bottle also indicates that the wine is made of 100% Ontario grapes of the type specified on the label. In 2000, the VQA Act was proclaimed into law in Ontario and the VQAO has become the authority regulating the use of the VQA label on wines in the province (www.wineroute.com/Ifacts.html). The 1990s saw the rapid growth of the number of wineries, which went from 18 in 1989 to 55 VQA producing wineries today. In Ontario there are now over 90 winery licenses issued in the province, which also includes cottage fruit wineries. Provincial liquor regulations restrict the sale of wine off site and as a result, the wineries must also attract as many visitors as possible to increase cellar door sales.

The wineries are represented by the Wine Council of Ontario (WCO), a non-profit trade association that acts as a liaison and co-ordinating body between Ontario wineries, grape growers, and government. It also assists in setting standards and establishing policy and future directions for the wine industry (www.wineroute.com/Ifacts. html). Currently, there are 12,000 acres of wine grapes in Ontario and Ontario wine represents 40% for the total wine market in Ontario. Total retail value of Ontario wine sales in 2000-01 was CDN $338 million and there was 41 million litres produced. In 2000-01, the total volume of VQA Ontario wines sold was 7,845,000 litres and in the same time frame, the sales of VQA Ontario wines represent 20% of total retail sales. A product, which Ontario is rapidly becoming known for, is Icewine. In the year 2000, Ontario produced 329,000 litres of Icewine (www.wineroute.com/Ifacts.html).

With the growing number of wineries and the increase in quality of Niagara wine brought about by the changes indicated above, there has been a corresponding growth in the number of tourists following the wine route. Both inbound and local tour operators also saw the opportunity and designed travel itineraries for coach tours that include winery visits. This quiet rise in wine tourism in the Niagara Region coincides with the Federal and Provincial governments' focus on culinary tourism as a new product to diversify Canadian tourism. In fact it can be argued that the initiatives which have taken place in the Niagara region have led the provincial and national tourism organizations in Canada to take notice of wine and culinary tourism and start to use these industries in their marketing strategies.

FOOD AND WINE MARKETING STRATEGIES

Recognizing the growing importance of the wine and culinary sectors, the Provincial government and the wine, culinary and tourism industry jointly funded the recently released Wine and Culinary Tourism Action Plan (CDN $243,000 and CDN $337,000 respectively). The overall vision of the plan is to establish Ontario as a quality wine and culinary tourism destination for both the domestic and international market. The plan offers specific strategies for Niagara and for Toronto, which are seen as the two main wine and culinary destinations. The report makes several recommendations for Niagara and few of these are highlighted here. The first is to establish an annual internationally recognized signature event aimed at raising the Niagara Region's profile as an international quality wine destination and to attract high yield visitors. The second recommendation is to enhance the experience on the Niagara Wine Route, which includes better signage, a better map and new information guides. One of the interesting recommendations of this report of particular relevance for this study is the suggestion to develop two sub-brands under the Wine Route brand, with one for "Niagara-on-the-Lake" and the other for the "Escarpment." These two suggested brands are closely aligned with the distinctions of west for the "Escarpment" and east for "Niagara-on-the-Lake" that are made in this paper when examining the results of the survey below. The attempt is being made to create an international market branding of Ontario as a premier wine and culinary tourism destination based on Niagara and Toronto (EPG, 2002). This new plan complements the recently released 20-year, CDN $20 million Ontario Wine Strategy, which charts the future of wine industry in the Province. The other local marketing partnership of note is that the wineries in Niagara-on-the-Lake have joined forces to form a Marketing Committee, which meets on a monthly basis. They have published joint marketing materials in hopes of establishing an identity as a cluster of wineries.

NIAGARA WINERY VISITOR STUDY

On weekends in July and August of 2000, visitors at eight of the Niagara Region wineries were interviewed. As outlined above, the Niagara Wine Route has two main clusters, the east and the west and four wineries were randomly selected in each cluster. While the wineries that were randomly selected varied in size, all have a tasting room for visitors. Researchers randomly approached visitors and those who agreed to participate are included in the data set. The researchers read the questions to the visitor and recorded their responses. A target of 50 completed surveys from each of the wineries was set and 406 valid surveys were obtained. Data collection varied in terms of time from one winery to another, depending on the number of visitors willing to complete the survey. The decision was made to not interview visitors in large tour groups as they often have very limited time at the winery. Some of the participants are, however, from smaller tour groups.

Data were analysed and compared by the location of the wineries (west vs. east). The questionnaire consisted of over 100 variables. In order to test the researchers' assumption that the profile of the visitors to the wineries in the west and the wineries in the east are different, an independent t-test (2-tailed) was done on the appropriate variables. Correlation of the variables ("location of the winery" and a variable) was also examined as well as a chi-square test to confirm that the variables are independent.

The visitors to the wineries in the west and the wineries in the east share many features. The following are some of the selected features that illustrate part of the visitor profile. The majority of them are Canadians (west 83%; east 61%) from the province of Ontario (west 94.7%; east 88.2%). It is the first visit to that particular winery for the large proportion of the visitors (west 63.2%; east 74.6%). The highest response categories

for the average amount of money they spend on wine at the winery is between $1-$25 range (west 26.9%; east 29.9%) and $26-$50 range (west
29.1%; east 21.0%). Similarly, their average monthly purchase of wine is
$11-20 range (west 17%; east 14.7%) and $21-$30 range (west 14.8%;
east 15.2%). All visitors equally evaluated purchase of wine, tasting, day
out, socialisation, a learning experience, relaxation, and meeting wine
makers as important factors to visit a winery. They also share the opinion
that the winery's cleanliness, environment, display of goods, smell inside
the building, architecture of the building as important attributes to visit a
winery. Their expectation from the wineries as a service provider is also
similar. They weigh factors such as winery staff's friendliness, service
provision, courteousness, knowledge, professional attitudes, and believ-
ability quite high. The entertainment at the winery is, however, considered to be less important. One interesting point to note: the visitors to the
wineries in the west show a slightly different attitude towards attributes
of wine, though statistically insignificant differences, from the visitors to
the wineries in the east. That is, the visitors to the west tend to place more
emphasis on taste, price, aroma, region, quality of wine, and being VQA,
than the visitors to the east.

Although the most of the profile of the winery visitors are similar,
there are several distinctively different features identified in Table 1.
The factors were isolated by t-test (2-tail significance). The summary of
significant profiles identified by t-test is shown in Table 2.

In summary, the visitors to the wineries in the west tend to buy wine
at the wineries while the visitors to the winery in the east tend to buy
wine at the retail outlets (LCBO, supermarkets, specialty wine shops).
This tendency may be explained by the next profile, which identified
that more visitors to the west have favorite varieties of wine. As sales of
wine at the retail outlets is strictly regulated by the government in Ontario, very limited varieties of Niagara wine are available, meanwhile
cellar door sales can offer wider varieties. Therefore, the visitors who
have a specific preference may have to visit the winery to purchase their
favourite kind of wine, and this may be the case of the visitors to the
west. Those visitors to the west also purchase more non-wine items
while visiting the winery. Many wineries today also sell wine accesso-
ries such as cheese-and-wine related items, souvenir items with grape
motifs and winery logos, food items and so on (Telfer, 2001a). Thus the
visitors to the wineries in the west are not only looking for wines.

More visitors to the wineries in the west have visited wineries in
other parts of Canada, in comparison to the visitors to the wineries in the
east. Even though the percentage of the visitors may not look signifi-

TABLE 1. T-Test for Equality of Means

	t	df	Sig. (2-tailed)
Where do you buy most of your wine?	-3.416	402	.001
Do you have any particular favourite variety of wine?	-3.034	400	.003
Have you ever purchased any souvenirs of non-wine products while visiting a winery?	-3.058	401	.002
Have you visited wineries in other part of Canada?	-3.465	401	.001
Factors to visit the winery today–tour	3.267	387	.001
Factors to visit the winery today–eating	-3.644	388	.000
Winery services–tour guide	2.609	390	.009
From the Niagara Region?	-4.816	396	.000
How many people (including yourself) are you visiting the winery with today?	2.841	394	.005
Are you visiting other tourist attractions in the Niagara Region today?	6.694	393	.000
What type of accommodation are you staying in?	4.254	375	.000
Eating out	-2.638	386	.009

cantly different, however, it could be summarized that the visitors to the wineries in the west are more avid visitors to wineries in general. Those visitors to the west do not seem to put weight on the winery tour when visiting wineries. Similarly the visitors to the east tend to consider the tour guide of the winery more important as part of the service at the winery than the visitors to the west. This may be perhaps that the visitors to the wineries in the east are less familiar with the wineries they are visiting, and the winery tour with a good tour guide is an important aspect of enjoying their visit.

One of the most significant differences between the visitors to the east and the west is the reason why they were visiting the winery on that day. The visitors to the west are coming to the wineries for "eating" (brunch, lunch, dinner, coffee or picnic). Amongst the wineries that participated in the survey, one winery in the west and one in the east have reputable on-site restaurants and some other wineries have picnic facilities. However, it is noteworthy that the larger proportion of the visitors in the west claim "eating" as the important component of the visitation to the winery. This is also reflected in the question how often the respondents dine out. More visitors in the west dine out "frequently" (west 69.5%; east 56.5%) while the visitors to the east dine out "often" (west 21.3%; east 28.0%). The winery in the west with the restaurant is more difficult to get to and off the main tourist route so there may be a strong tendency for those visiting this winery to be going there specifically for the restaurant.

TABLE 2. Summary of Cross-Tabulation (by area)

Where do you buy most of your wine? (% within "by area")

	West	East
on site at the winery	**31.5%**	10.3%
LCBO	48.1%	55.6%
super market	5.0%	**11.7%**
speciality wine shop	7.7%	**13.9%**

Chi-Square Tests: Asymp. Sig. (2-sided), .000   Spearman Correlation: Value .245, Approx. Sig., .000

Do you have any particular favourite variety of wine? (% within "by area")

	West	East
yes	**77.2%**	65.8%
no	19.4%	**23.9%**
no answer	3.3%	10.4%

Chi-Square Tests: Asymp. Sig. (2-sided), .009   Spearman Correlation: Value, .137, Approx. Sig., .006

Have you ever purchased any souvenirs of non-wine products while visiting a winery? (% within "by area")

	West	East
yes	**51.1%**	38.1%
no	47.2%	**56.1%**
no answer	1.7%	5.8%

Chi-Square Tests: Asymp. Sig. (2-sided), .008   Spearman Correlation: Value, .154, Approx. Sig., .004

Have you visited wineries in other part of Canada? (% within "by area")

	West	East
yes	**38.1%**	21.6%
no	59.1%	**74.8%**
no answer	2.8%	3.6%

Chi-Square Tests: Asymp. Sig. (2-sided), .001   Spearman Correlation: Value, .175, Approx. Sig., .000

Factors to visit the winery today–tour (% within "by area")

	West	East
very important	10.7%	**19.9%**
important	12.4%	**16.6%**
somewhat important	**16.3%**	13.7%
not so important	**18.5%**	14.2%
not important	16.3%	**23.7%**
not important at all	16.3%	8.1%

Chi-Square Tests: Asymp. Sig. (2-sided), .002   Spearman Correlation: Value −.158, Approx. Sig., .002

TABLE 2 (continued)

Factors to visit the winery today–eating (% within "by area")

	West	East
very important	**17.4%**	4.7%
important	**16.3%**	9.0%
somewhat important	14.0%	11.8%
not so important	18.0%	**25.9%**
not important	15.2%	**35.4%**
not important at all	12.9%	10.8%
no answer	6.2%	2.4%

Chi-Square Tests: Asymp. Sig. (2-sided), .000   Spearman Correlation: Value .174, Approx. Sig., .001

Winery services–tour guide (% within "by area")

	West	East
very important	18.1%	**36.7%**
important	**24.9%**	19.1%
somewhat important	19.8%	12.6%
not so important	11.9%	10.2%
not important	7.9%	10.2%
not important at all	10.7%	6.0%
no answer	6.8%	5.1%

Chi-Square Tests: Asymp. Sig. (2-sided), .002   Spearman Correlation: Value –.157, Approx. Sig., .002

Are you from the Niagara Region? (% within "by area")

	West	East
yes	**23.9%**	7.3%
no	76.1%	**92.2%**

Chi-Square Tests: Asymp. Sig. (2-sided), .000   Spearman Correlation: Value .235, Approx. Sig., .000

How many people including yourself are you visiting the winery with today?

	West	East
1	2.2%	1.4%
2	46.1%	**61.5%**
3-5	**39.3%**	31.7%
5-10	6.7%	3.2%
10-15	.6%	.5%
15-20	1.1%	.5%
over 20	2.8%	.5%

Chi-Square Tests: Asymp. Sig. (2-sided), .070   Spearman Correlation: Value –.150, Approx. Sig., .003

What type of accommodation are you staying in?

	West	East
with family/friend	**17.4%**	14.1%
hotel/motel	14.0%	**30.2%**
bed and breakfast	5.8%	**18.0%**
camping	2.9%	3.9%
other	15.1%	11.7%
no answer	44.8%	22.0%

Chi-Square Tests: Asymp. Sig. (2-sided), .000   Spearman Correlation: Value − .196, Approx. Sig., .000

Eating out

	West	East
frequently	**69.5%**	56.5%
often	21.3%	**28.0%**
sometimes	6.3%	7.0%
rarely	.6%	2.8%
never		1.9%

Chi-Square Tests: Asymp. Sig. (2-sided), .052   Spearman Correlation: Value .140, Approx. Sig. .006

The last important difference in the visitor profile is that the visitors to the west tend to be more local (23.9%), while the visitors to the east are from outside the region (92.2%). This has a implications for repeat visits to wineries. In addition, the visitors to the wineries in the west seem to come in larger groups (3-5 people) than the visitors to the east (2 people). This, however, must be placed in the context that members of large groups were often not approached for the survey. The question about the type of accommodation suggest that the visitors to the wineries in the east are from outside the region and stay at commercial establishments such as hotels, motels and B&Bs. Unfortunately this question did not probe whether or not the visitors to the west are excursionists/day trippers from the Niagara Region and do not require commercial accommodation.

IMPLICATIONS FOR MARKETING STRATEGIES ON THE NIAGARA WINE ROUTE

With the different markets emerging in the Region, wineries need to be aware of who their main market segments are. In terms of the international market, efforts have been already made to market to the Japanese tourists directly. Individual wineries have made linkages with Japanese tour operators giving the tour groups discounts on wine tasting. Inniskillin winery, for example, has packaged its Icewine in small sampler bottles, which are easy to carry and represent a valuable gift for the Japanese tourist to take back as a souvenir (Hashimoto & Telfer, 1999). The wineries in the east, which currently attract more international group visitors, primarily due to location, need to continue to be adaptable to different customs and establish links with tour operators who will place the winery on the tour itinerary. Continued efforts need to be taken to recognise the domestic market. In fact, many of the tourists to the wineries in the west cluster could be classified more as day-trippers or local area visitors as opposed to tourists. It will continue to be important to develop strategies to promote brand loyalty for these local customers as a way of maintaining repeat visitors. As Dodd (2000) suggests, gathering marketing information and developing long-term relationships with visitors will continue to be an important activity for wineries. With more and more wineries coming on line, there will be an increasing need for the wineries to distinguish themselves from one and other. While the style of wine produced at the winery will always be the main determinant for visitors, other products and services provided by a winery will also help to differentiate one from the other. The introduction of restaurants, cooking schools and various special events can be used as marketing tools to help get people to the winery. For instance, in the case of Niagara, the survey results revealed that visitors to the wineries in the west tend to be more local and food and wine connoisseurs, and do not value other entertainment as high as those visitors to the wineries in the east. Therefore, the wineries in the west should focus on retaining their current clients by offering special food-and-wine events, but not necessarily unrelated concerts or entertainment. They could also consider marketing to independent international visitors. For those wineries the Chinese, Japanese or German tourists who are well-known for their organized coach travel may not be the best market. Meanwhile the wineries in the east that have capacities to accommodate coach tourists could establish and maintain linkages, for example, with inbound tour operators for the Chinese, Japanese and German tourists. However smaller wineries in the east may want to market to more local visitors by providing special events or by offering special deals for local and repeat clients. One winery in the east, not included in this survey, has started a barrel club program where people can put money towards the purchase of an oak wine barrel, which is used at the winery. Their name is placed on the barrel and they are invited to special events for those only in the barrel club.

In addition to getting a better understanding of who their market is, wineries also need to be aware of some of the positive and negative implications for marketing at different geographic levels. Figure 1 indicates some of the potential advantages and disadvantages of different marketing scales. As wine is very much tied to a geographic location, wineries can use this to their advantage. As the geographic scope of the marketing image expands, so too does the potential positives and negatives accrue. A winery for example can choose to market on its own or it can also choose to market jointly with the wineries in its immediate cluster. The wineries in Niagara-on-the-Lake for example have joined forces to form a Marketing Committee and they all contribute financially to selected marketing campaigns. All of the wineries also take part in festivals celebrating the Niagara Wine Route such as the Niagara Grape and Wine Festival. At the provincial level, the Wine Council of Ontario and the Provincial Ministry responsible for tourism is assisting in marketing Ontario Wines. At the national level, the Canadian Tourism Commission has been providing the support to market Canada as a wine and culinary destination. Beginning in 1999, the Canadian Tourism Commission in partnership with industry hosted a series of eight Regional Round Tables on culinary tourism (St. John's, Charlottetown, Vancouver, Niagara Falls, Saskatoon, Winnipeg, Edmonton and Montreal) (MacDonald and Deneault, 2001) which led to the recent publication of the Canadian Tourism Commission's Product Development Strategy for Cuisine Tourism (Deneault, 2002). One of the recommendations in this report is that the Canadian Tourism Commission Product Development Group will "assist in influencing the branding, marketing opportunities and market development of culinary tourism in Canada" (Deneault, 2002, 10). The benefits associated with expanding the geographic scope of the marketing are highlighted in Figure 1 as there are increasing economies of scale generated as well as being recognised as part of a wider brand. On the other hand, there are associated costs of expanding the scope of the marketing as increasingly complex partnerships are generated and there is a loss of individual winery identity in marketing at a much broader geographic scope. How well the partnership works and the level of control a winery has inside the partnership will determine how much they benefit from these partnerships. It is however becoming more important especially for the smaller wineries to take advantage of these types of partnerships (Telfer, 2001a; Hall, 2002).

CONCLUSIONS

The Niagara Wine Route has been transformed in the last twenty years and is rapidly establishing itself as a New World Wine Route, up and coming on the global scene. The image of the Niagara Region is

FIGURE 1. Advantages and Disadvantages of Different Geographic Wine Marketing Levels

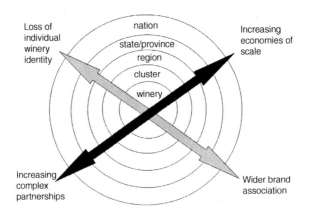

changing from being solely focused on Niagara Falls itself to one that includes the wine route. Marketing efforts have been taken with the development of the Wine and Culinary Tourism Action Plan funded jointly by the Provincial government and the wine, culinary and tourism industry. This new plan complements the new 20-year, CDN $20 million Ontario Wine Strategy also recently released. Within these developments it is important for wineries to understand who their markets are and recognize that wineries within the wine route may have different customer profiles. The research presented here indicates that the wineries in the east have a greater potential to attract international visitors than those wineries in the west primarily due to location.

With respect to marketing there are several issues that can be addressed with the issue of scale. As indicated in Figure 1, at the scale of the entire wine route, there is the importance of getting the image out about Niagara Wine. It is still in its infancy; however, it has made major gains in the last twenty years. Below the level of the entire wine route are the two main wine clusters. The wineries in the east have formed the Niagara-on-the-Lake Wine Marketing Committee, which meets to develop marketing strategies. In the west, initial meetings have taken place with assistance from the Ontario Tourism Marketing Partnership program. Below the cluster level are the individual wineries, which have to decide at what level they want to partner with other wineries to market. This is clearly an area requiring greater attention. One future research project would include an analysis of the visitors who arrive at the winery on a large tour bus to determine their attitudes and preferences towards Niagara wine. While there are many similarities between visitors to the west and visitors to the east, understanding the subtle differences between the groups may help to better position a winery in the increasingly competitive market place.

REFERENCES

Cambourne, B., Macionis, N, Hall, C.M. & Sharples, L. (2000). The future of wine tourism. In C. M. Hall, L. Sharples, B. Cambourne & N. Macionis (Eds.). *Wine and Tourism From Around the World.* London: Butterworth Heinemann, 297-320.

Chapman, P. (1994). Agriculture in Niagara: An overview. In H. Gayler (Ed.) *Niagara's Changing Landscapes.* Ottawa: Carleton University Press, 297-300.

Deneault, M. (2002). *Acquiring a Taste for Cuisine Tourism: A Product Development Strategy.* Canadian Tourism Commission.

Dodd, T. (2000). Influences on cellar door sales and determinants of wine tourism success: Results from Texas wineries. In C. M. Hall, L. Sharples, B. Cambourne & N. Macionis (Eds.). *Wine and Tourism from Around the World.* London: Butterworth Heinemann, 136-149.

Economic Planning Group of Canada (EPG) (2002). *Wine and Culinary Tourism in Ontario–Executive Summary.* Ottawa: Economic Planning Group of Canada.

Getz, D. (2000). *Explore Wine Tourism: Management, Development & Destinations.* New York: Cognizant Communications Corporations.

Hall, C.M. (1996). Wine tourism in New Zealand. In G. Kearsley (Ed.). *Tourism down under II, towards a more sustainable tourism, conference proceedings.* (pp. 109-119). Dunedin, NZ: Centre for Tourism, University of Otago, Dunedin.

Hall, C.M. (2002). Local initiatives for local regional development: The role of food, wine and tourism. In E. Arola, J, Kärkkäinen & M. Siitari (Eds.). *Tourism and Well Being* (pp. 47-63). The 2nd Tourism Industry and Education Symposium, held at Jyväskylä Polytechnic, Jyväskylä, Finland (May 16-18, 2002).

Hall, C.M., Johnson, G., Cambourne, B. Macionis, N., Mitchell, R. & Sharples, L. (2000). Wine tourism: An introduction. In C.M. Hall, L. Sharples, B. Cambourne & N. Macionis (Eds.). *Wine and Tourism From Around the World.* London: Butterworth Heinemann, 1-23.

Hashimoto, A. & Telfer, D.J. (1999). Marketing Icewine to Japanese tourists in Niagara: The case of Inniskillin Winery. *International Journal of Wine Marketing,* 11(2), 29-41.

Kotler, P., Haider, D. & Rein, I. (1993). *Marketing Places: Attracting Investment, Industry and Tourism to Cities, States and Nations.* New York: The Free Press.

Kotler, P. et al. (1999). *Principles of Marketing* 2nd Edition. London: Prentice Hall.

MacDonald, H. & Deneault, M. (2001). *National Tourism & Cuisine Forum: "Recipes for Success"–Proceedings and Final Report.* Canadian Tourism Commission.

Macionis, N. (1996). Wine tourism in Australia. In G. Kearsley (Ed.). *Tourism down under II, towards a more sustainable tourism, conference proceedings.* (pp. 264-286). Dunedin, NZ: Centre for Tourism, University of Otago, Dunedin.

Middleton, V.C. (1994). *Marketing in Travel and Tourism* 2nd Edition. Oxford: Butterworth-Heinemann.

Mitchell, R. & Hall, C.M. (2001). The influence of gender and region on the New Zealand winery visit. *Tourism Recreation Research*, 26(2), 63-75.

Mitchell, R., Hall, C.M. & McIntosh, A. (2000). Wine tourism and consumer behavior. In C. M. Hall, L. Sharples, B. Cambourne & N. Macionis (Eds.). *Wine and Tourism from Around the World*. London: Butterworth Heinemann, 115-135.

Peters, G.L. (1997). *American Winescapes*. Boulder: Westview Press.

Swarbrooke, J. & Horner, S. (1999). *Consumer Behavior in Tourism*. Oxford: Butterworth-Heinemann.

Telfer, D.J. (2001a). Strategic alliances along the Niagara Wine Route. *Tourism Management*, 22(1), 21-30.

Telfer, D.J. (2001b). From a Wine Tourism village to a regional wine route: An investigation of the competitive advantage of embedded clusters in Niagara, Canada. *Tourism Recreation Research*, 26(2), 23-33.

Telfer, D.J. (2000a). The Northeast Wine Route: Wine Tourism in Ontario, Canada and New York State. In C.M. Hall, L. Sharples, B. Cambourne & N. Macionis (Eds.). *Wine and Tourism From Around the World*. London: Butterworth Heinemann, 253-271.

Telfer, D.J. (2000b). Tastes of Niagara: Building strategic alliances between tourism and agriculture. In J. Crotts, D. Buhalis & R. March (Eds.). *Global Alliances in Tourism and Hospitality Management*. London: The Haworth Hospitality Press, 71-88.

Telfer, D.J. & Hashimoto, A. (2000). Niagara Icewine tourism: Japanese souvenir purchases at Inniskillin Winery. *Tourism and Hospitality Research: The Surrey Quarterly Review*, 2(4), 343-356.

www.wineroute.com/Ifacts.html. *The Ontario Wine Industry*.

An Analysis of Regional Positioning and Its Associated Food Images in French Tourism Regional Brochures

Isabelle Frochot

SUMMARY. The image of France has often been associated with that of food and wines and images of food products, vineyards and restaurants have traditionally dominated national and regional promotional strategies and tour operators' brochures alike. Indeed, food represents a powerful eye-catcher and a strong symbol of quality of life and authenticity, as a result it has represented an important theme used in advertisements. However, the food theme is in fact multiple and can also be used to portray symbols of cultural identify, communication and status. Therefore, the present study first aims at identifying the different food images that can be used by tourism advertisers in their promotional material. Secondly the study aims at investigating how different food images can be used for specific destinations' positioning strategies. The research uses a content analysis to identify the types of food images used in 19 French regional tourism brochures. Results show that country products/dishes and raw/natural products dominate food images followed by wine and vineyards images. Images of food producers, chefs, restaurants and the presence of people in the pictures on the other side are

Isabelle Frochot is affiliated with Université de Savoie, BP 1104, 73011 Chambéry Cedex, France (E-mail: Isabelle.frochot@univ-savoie.fr).

[Haworth co-indexing entry note]: "An Analysis of Regional Positioning and Its Associated Food Images in French Tourism Regional Brochures." Frochot, Isabelle. Co-published simultaneously in *Journal of Travel & Tourism Marketing* (The Haworth Hospitality Press, an imprint of The Haworth Press, Inc.) Vol. 14, No. 3/4, 2003, pp. 77-96; and: *Wine, Food, and Tourism Marketing* (ed: C. Michael Hall) The Haworth Hospitality Press, an imprint of The Haworth Press, Inc., 2003, pp. 77-96. Single or multiple copies of this article are available for a fee from The Haworth Document Delivery Service [1-800-HAWORTH, 9:00 a.m. - 5:00 p.m. (EST). E-mail address: docdelivery@haworthpress.com].

10.1300/J073v14n03_05

underrepresented. Parallels between the categories of food images used in brochures and the corresponding positioning strategies chosen by the regions are not very strong. Nevertheless, the study indicates that regions that position themselves on the traditional/rural/authentic theme use mostly images of raw products, country products and market scenes while only a few regions position themselves on the gastronomy dimension. In other terms, the cultural dimension of food as an identity marker for the regions is its principal use, and images of food associated to communicating/sharing or to status/lifestyle statements are rarely used in French regional brochures. *[Article copies available for a fee from The Haworth Document Delivery Service: 1-800-HAWORTH. E-mail address: <docdelivery@haworthpress.com> Website: <http://www.HaworthPress.com> © 2003 by The Haworth Press, Inc. All rights reserved.]*

KEYWORDS. Image, France, wine tourism, brochures

INTRODUCTION

The image of France has often been associated with that of a country of culture, fashion, romanticism and, above all, a gastronomic and wine producing country. Among all these icons, food has been a recurring theme in France's tourism promotional strategy both on domestic and international markets. As examples, the latest promotional campaign for "Gîtes de France" (rural accommodation) on the British market constituted of a range of seven pictures of countryside market stalls (portraying cheeses, countryside products, vegetables and wines). Similarly, the French destination marketing organization, Maison de la France, launched a promotional campaign in 2001 called "Give your taste buds a holiday too!" which featured pictures of raw seafood on a sea background. Equally, the Eurostar campaign "From fish and chips to Moules et frites" featured a picture of mussels while the shuttle campaign used the sole picture of a vineyard to promote a transport connection. Taken together these types of advertisements attest of the recurrent use of the food theme in tourism advertisements in order to portray an image of France linked to good foods and lifestyle.

Nevertheless, beyond the imagery of food and its powerful theming in advertisements, food and wine represent also a significant tourism asset for tourists visiting the country. However, among all tourists' products, food and wine is one that is most difficult to study since it is often provided by a variety of local micro-private actors whose coordination towards the creation of regional/national tourism products can be difficult. Although France has developed different schemes to coordinate those actors (food and wine trails, regional promotional schemes of local dishes, food and wine festivals), these actions are often undertaken at a local/regional level and no national plan in food and wine tourism promotion exists (Frochot, 2000). Furthermore, to date, few initiatives have taken place in this field apart from some interesting projects developed in the new world (Australia and New Zealand for instance) where food and wine tourism has been formalized and efficiently organised at a regional/national tourism strategy level (Hall et al., 2000). But beyond practical developments, academia lacks studies which attempting at understanding the connections between food, destination images, and food products at destinations: ". . . discussion of the Troika of tourism, food, identity is surprisingly limited given the extent to which food is used in destination and place promotion" (Hall and Mitchell, 2000, p. 34). This lack of research is partly due to the late recognition that food and wine can be efficiently linked to tourism but also because it is a topic particularly difficult to research and evaluate.

This lack of research can be explained in part by several factors. First of all, most existing surveys, and particularly those conducted in France, do not allow visitors to indicate the extent and/or the importance of food and wine in their holiday experience (most questions listed in visitors' surveys concentrate on their consumption of heritage and their leisure activities). Furthermore, one problem with food tourism research is the failure of existing studies and surveys to distinguish between an activity that is both necessary and pleasurable to holidaymakers. Indeed, food is primarily a physiological need that is situated at the basic survival level of any individual's life. However, if the survival issue does not fully apply to tourists, it remains that food is a necessity that holidaymakers need to fulfil while travelling. At the same time, food also represents one of the most pleasurable activities that holidaymakers will undertake when visiting a country. However, most existing studies do not distinguish in their statistics those two dimensions of food consumption. In fact this distinction might have two implications: on one side because food is also a necessity, during a trip as well as in everyday life, this element might not transpire in surveys as it is considered as a "logical" element of a trip and therefore tourists might take it for granted when evaluating a tourism offering. Secondly, it implies that it is not necessarily because people will engage into various food encounters during their trip that they will necessarily consider them as substantial components of their holiday experience. For instance, a recent study on rural tourists to Scotland (Frochot and McLellan, 2002) clearly identified that food was ranked as the third activity most undertaken by tourists but when those were asked to rate their preferred activities, food and drink only came in sixth position. The lack of studies identifying this difference is clearly a shortcoming that has restricted the understanding of the role of food in tourism developments.

The second problem encountered in food tourism studies is the complex relationship between the food image of a destination and the activities undertaken while at the destination. Indeed, it is important to recognize that while food and wine can represent a strong icon and to this effect an important theme to promote a country, it is often by far not the principal activity undertaken by tourists when visiting that country. Indeed, in the case of France the prime activity of international visitors remains the visit of heritage attractions followed by beach activities and social interactions (Secrétariat d'Etat au Tourisme, 1998). This of course is partly due to the lack of integration of activities relating to food in survey questions but it also translates the fact that drinking and feeding oneself cannot in themselves represent all-day activities. Indeed, even in wine producing regions, heritage remains the prime activity of visitors hence suggesting that wine is mostly considered as a complementary and pleasurable activity to existing destinations' tourists assets: "Food is the theme of additional tourist activities in regions and enterprises whose core products are something else" (Hjalager and Corigliano, 2000, p. 282). Williams (2001), in a study of wine images in Canada, has also noted the increasing use in wine tourism brochures of other tourist/leisurely recreational pursuits. Equally, the development of wine trails that integrate in their design visits to various heritage monuments and tourists sites testify to this secondary role (Frochot, 2000). In other words, food and wine represent a strong unifying theme for a tourism product but probably not its core appeal.

However, research has identified that food can represent an important source of satisfaction for visitors (Ryan, 1997; Smith, 1983). For instance, food service has been categorised as the fourth most important contributor to visitors' satisfaction and the most important influential factor upon intentions to return in a study on Turkey (Rimmington and Yüksel, 1998). Furthermore, food has also been identified as the fourth most important attribute for tourists' perceptions of destination attractiveness after climate, accommodation and scenery (Hu and Ritchie, 1993). In another study on several countries, Jenkins (1999) identified that different cuisine/food/drink came in ninth position and hospitality and friendliness of local inhabitants came second in destination selection. Acheson (1990) also identified that food might play an important role but only in certain circumstances: "food plays little or no part in the choice of a holiday destination, except for individual travellers to countries like France, Italy or more distantly, India, where it may well be an integral part of the holiday experience" (p. 225). If these studies tend to show different results, often depending of the countries studied, they do nevertheless attest of the importance of food and wine in tourists' satisfaction and destination selection.

The last recognized limit to existing food studies is linked to the complexity of the food theme since one cannot refer to food and wine as a single theme. Indeed, the complexity of the food theme lies with the different meaning that it can take: "Food means more than eating. Food relates to issues of identity, culture, production, consumption and, increasingly, issues of sustainability" (Hall and Mitchell, 2000, p. 29). This is precisely this multifaceted aspect of food which is central to the present article since it indicates that food images can potentially be used to imply different meanings and interpretations. This multiple meaning of food has been addressed by several authors who have identified that food consumption could portray four different symbolic meanings. First, beyond its nutritious, hygienic and psychosensorial qualities, food can only exist (i.e., be accepted as such) if it is culturally accepted by the inhabitants of a region/country (Bourdieu, 1979). The dislike of some Asian countries for cheese, the British visitors' repulsion for snails or the undeserved dislike of French people for Scottish haggis testify that food is before everything else a culturally learned endeavour: "Men do not eat what they like, they eat what they are used to" (Bourdieu, 1979, p. 345).

Secondly, food can represent an icon since it constitutes an identity for inhabitants of a region/nation, an icon to which they can identify as a common cultural unifying trait (Bourdieu, 1979; Ryan, 1997). Of course this also implies that food can represent a strong identifying theme in tourism promotion: "Food is therefore intimately tied up with the production and consumption of the cultural meaning of place and space" (Hall and Mitchell, 2000, p. 35). This is particularly true in France where the identity of its regions is tightly linked to the local production of specific food products, wines and regional cuisine.

Thirdly, food can represent a social class indicator (champagne, caviar, whisky are all strong identity markers for upper social classes). To an extent, countries can also compete on this theme by providing status images in their promotion through either the products/gastronomy experiences they are offering or simply the ways in which those are consumed. It is for instance evident that for British, American and Dutch visitors to France, the visit of cellars and purchase of wines, the purchase of second homes, and simply the knowledge of local cooking can be used by those tourists to affirm their status.

Finally, food is closely associated to communication as, the ways in which food is eaten and shared represent a fundamental social bond (Poulain, 1996; Ryan, 1997). In this sense, the word "consumption" can also mean literally the absorption of a cultural identity, by immersing with the local culture. By eating local food, by sharing it with local inhabitants, by adapting to different eating manners, the tourist is not only a spectator but he/she also becomes an actor of that culture and can achieve greater communication with local inhabitants than he would otherwise (Poulain, 2000).

In summary, it can be expressed that food images (and consumption) can be used to portray images of cultural experience, status, cultural identity, and communicating/sharing. However, beyond those qualities, one can clearly see that most of the existing motivations pertaining to tourism consumption can be experienced through a culinary experience. Indeed, food tourism can also be conceptualized as allowing tourists to achieve relaxation (relaxing in a restaurant or at the terrace of a café), excitement (trying new food, new ways of eating), escapism (changing from the usual food/everyday life), status (trying some expensive or different food), education (increasing one's knowledge about different types of food and wine and how to cook them), lifestyle (the simple fact to be outside in nice weather and enjoying nice wine and food). In other words, most of the colours of the tourist motivational palette can be achieved through the consumption of food (Hjalager and Corigliano, 2000; Rimmington and Yüksel, 1998).

Consequently the present research argues that food tourism, because of this diversity, can be considered as a specific tool through which destinations can ascertain their cultural uniqueness and affirm their positioning strategy. This is particularly important since it can be used by destinations as a tool to reduce their risk of substitutability with other destinations (Hall and Mitchell, 2000; Sancton and Le Quesne, 2001). In other words, food and wine can allow destinations to increase the uniqueness of their identity and thereby position themselves more clearly in the eyes of customers and in comparison to other destinations. The notion of uniqueness has already been addressed by several researchers (Pearce, 1982, Echtner and Ritchie, 1993) who argued that destination uniqueness can be represented via symbols or atmospheres that are perceived as being unique to that destination. As a result, destinations positioning strategies and image reinforcement are increasingly focussing on promoting uniqueness and holistic and emotional appeal rather than simply recognisable physical attributes. In the present case, the food image in France can be analyzed both as a unique physical attribute (French food and cooking reputation, specificity of markets, wine producing areas, cheeses, etc.) but also as a common psychological/emotional or holistic attribute (the French "art de vivre," informal cafés and ways of eating, real contact with people, lifestyle statement, etc.). It is therefore important to appreciate how food images and positioning strategies can be linked.

METHODOLOGY

The first objective of the research was to identify the range and diversity of food and wine images that are used in French tourism regional brochures. The second objective was then to draw parallels between those images and the positioning strategies of the regions to appreciate to which extent those two aspects could be linked. Therefore, the study aimed at evaluating how specific food images could be used to ascertain the positioning of a region.

In order to achieve these two objectives, the research involved a content analysis of visual imagery of French regional tourism brochures. The brochures selected were those produced for the summer of 2002 by 19 French regions (for the other three regions, the brochures were not yet available). The brochures were those published by the regional public tourism organizations and as such represented the "essence" that these regions wished to portray to potential tourists. Brochures were used as opposed to other promotional tools since they had been recognised as "the most popular medium used by travel and tourism advertisers . . . the brochure is arguably the key image-creating tool in tourism" (Morgan and Pritchard, 2000, p. 65). The use of content analysis was substantiated by its extensive and efficient applications notably when analyzing the pictures used in advertisements or brochures by the tourism industry (Dann, 1996; Mellinger, 1994; Pritchard and Morgan, 1996; Williams, 2001). Its usefulness had also been well recognised: "Content analysis of written information, such as guidebooks or visual information including photographs in travel brochures, can provide a great deal of information about the images projected of tourist destinations" (Jenkins, 1999, p. 8). As with every technique, particularly of a qualitative nature, shortcomings have also been identified such as the limits encountered in providing a clear definition of the topic searched, difficulties in identifying a measurable unit of the study and usual problems of impending subjectivity (Berger, 1998).

In order to improve the objectivity of the analysis an expert panel of five tourism academics was selected with the first aim to identify the positioning of each region. Positioning themes were identified through an evaluation of all the images presented in the brochures together with an integration of the slogan used by each region. Food and wine images were included in this analysis (despite the fact that they might influence the judgment) because gastronomy was seen as a potential tourist asset in itself by some regions (the fact that food and wine images displayed might have influenced the panel is a recognized shortcoming). First of all, the panel identified a range of 11 possible positioning themes from the brochures' images studied. For the simplicity of the analysis, they were requested to identify a maximum of two themes for the positioning of each region (this limited selection of themes was only used for the comparison of positioning with food images). The second role of the panel was then to identify the range and types of food images used in each regional brochure. It was seen as preferable, due to the lack of research on food images especially in France, not to use existing themes identified in previous research but rather to build a list upon the brochures used in the study. This analysis was conducted by using a content analysis approach of the images relating to food (the purpose was not to identify the place and extent of food images compared to other topics portrayed in the brochures but simply to concentrate on the food theme). The panel first identified a range of 16 food themes and then evaluated for each brochure the recurrence of the pictures reviewed for each theme.

FINDINGS

The first findings concerned the positioning of the regions.

The Positioning of the Regions

The panels first identified a range of 11 themes that were used by the different regions. Although some themes might be seen as redundant by the reader, their identification was clearly justified as will be expressed thereafter (those results are presented in Table 1).

The theme history was among the most common theme since most brochures had information pertaining to the heritage of their region (im-

TABLE 1. Positioning Themes Across All Regions

Theme	Proportion
Natural	19.8%
History	18.5%
Authentic	16%
Traditional	12.3%
Pure	8.6%
Rural	8.6%
Activities	4.9%
Arts and Crafts	4.9%
Wild	3.7%
Gastronomy	2.5%

ages of castles, museums, historic buildings, etc.), it represented 18.5% of all themes. With a similar occurrence was the theme of nature, most probably translating the latest trend for the outdoors and the desire from tourists to resource themselves in a natural environment (19.8% of all themes). However, the natural theme could also be associated to other themes such as wilderness (3.7%), in that case translating a very untouched and wild environment (the Pyrénées for instance). But it could also be associated to the theme of purity (8.6%), in this case implying still a natural environment but non-threatening (this theme was either used by mountainous regions or by regions along the Atlantic coast).

The rural theme was distinguished from those as it depicted rather the peaceful, relaxing and real image of the France countryside and contributed to 8.6% of all themes (images of villages, rolling and green countryside, farm animals and the infamous countryside markets). Close to the theme of rurality two other themes were identified, the first one was that of authenticity which referred to the real, genuine, simple and non-staged experiences that tourists could come across (portrays of local people in their work environment, architecture respectful of a local culture, real food products, etc.). A close theme was that of traditions (12.3%) which implied the cultural uniqueness of each region. This was slightly different than authenticity since it translated rather the wish by some French regions to perpetuate ancestral traditions and local customs (locals portrayed in their "folkloric" dresses, local events and sports typical of a region, specific musical instruments). Arts and crafts were also a minor theme, contributing to only 4.9% of all themes. The activities theme (4.9%) portrayed the range of activities that tourists could undertake while visiting the region (from canoeing to skiing, swimming, fishing, etc). Gastronomy was identified as the most minor theme since it represented 2.5% of all themes; this does not imply that it had the least proportion of images but the panel felt that very few regions openly used their gastronomy as an asset to attract tourists.

Analysis of the Food Images' Themes

Following the panel identification of the main positioning theme of each region, a content analysis of the brochures' images was then undertaken. As stated in the methodology, images pertaining to the food and wine theme were only retained in that part of the analysis, the objective being to identify the range of images used by the 19 regions and then compare those to their positioning strategies. The range of the food themes and their frequency of occurrence are presented in Table 2.

In terms of food products one of the most important categories was that of country dishes (cooked and presented in a country style such as in a rural dish, on a wooden table with no table cloth; often, these were homemade tarts, stews or soups). While those cooked country dishes accounted for 12.9% of all images, country products (dried cure ham, sausages, honey) also contributed to 6.2% of the images and cheeses to 7%. In adjunction, pictures of farm animals contributed to 5.2% of the pictures, market scenes to 4.5% and delicacies (locally produced food products such as sweets or specific cakes) to 3.2%. In summary all food products pertaining directly or indirectly to a rural lifestyle contributed

TABLE 2. Range of Food Themes Used

Food theme	Proportion
Unprepared/raw products	13.2%
Country dishes	12.9%
Vineyards	12.4%
Natural products	8%
Bottle of wine/glass of wine	8%
Cheeses	7%
Food trade	6.5%
Country product	6.2%
Farm animals	5.2%
Market	4.5%
Restaurant dish	4.2%
Delicacies	3.2%
Restaurant table set-up	3%
Restaurant/café with customers	4.5%
Wine cellar	1.2%

to the largest category of images (39%). For this analysis, the wine theme was analysed separately and contributed to an important coverage of the pictures since pictures of vineyards or grapes, wine cellars and picture of a wine bottle(s) with or without a glass made up 21.6% of all images. Unprepared or raw products (fruits in a bowl, raw seafood) constituted 13.2% of all images while "natural" products (products shown in their environment such as apples or berries on a tree, mushrooms in the soil) represented 8% of the images. These two categories on their own represented 21.2% of all pictures.

In regard to more "conventional" food production, the gastronomy and its associated chefs for which France is renowned, little evidence could be found of this aspect. In fact, the vast majority of food and wine images portrayed tended to show one or several food products on their own but very little evidence of their producers or of their consumers could be found. For instance, the "trade workers" category which grouped images of farmers, bakers, cooks, fishermen and winemakers was only the seventh most common image (6.5% of all pictures). It is also particularly important to note that within that category, chefs were underrepresented apart from the Riviera (the tradition of palaces) and in Burgundy (a gastronomic region by excellence) where a few pictures could be found. In fact, the majority of the pictures of food trade portrayed other professions, particularly bakers and fishermen.

Furthermore, pictures of restaurants were few and far between since pictures of restaurant or café scenes with people represented only 4.5 percent of all images. Finally, images of dishes on their own classically presented in a restaurant style (set up on a table cloth with glasses) contributed to 4.2% of images and tables set up for dinners but without people to 3% of images.

Food Images Used in Brochures and Positioning

Finally, the link between food images and positioning strategies was not easy to identify. There might be several reasons explaining this result. First of all, the lack of diversity in the food images used might explain the lack of potential linkages with positioning strategies (regions tended to use the same range of images). Secondly, the use of some food images can be linked to specific geographical characteristics as will be explained thereafter. Table 3 presents the frequency of occurrence of the food images (per category) for each region along with their most important positioning theme. Due to the lack of some pictures across different regions, statistical testing for differences was not operated

TABLE 3. Comparison of Food Images Used Per Region (and associated positioning)

Pictures	Limousin	Auvergne	Région-Centre	Aquitaine	Poitou-Charentes	Lorraine	Nord-Pas-de-Calais	Alsace	Normandie	Britanny	Languedoc-Rousillon	Picardie	Rhône-Alpes	Franche-Comté	Paris-IDF	Midi-Pyrénées	Pays de la Loire	Bourgogne	Côte-d'Azur	Total
Positioning	R/A	W/P	R/H	T/G	N/A	A/R	R/A	A/N	N/Ar	T/N	N/T	N/T	N/Ac	P/Ac	T/H	W/N	A/H	G/R	G/C	
Café/restaurant scene with people eating around a table	25	12.5	0	0	0	12.5	25	0	0	0	0	0	12.5	0	12.5	0	0	0	0	100
Dish cooked on its own, restaurant style	0	0	47	0	11	0	0	5.8	0	0	0	0	0	0	0	0	5.8	23.5	0	100
Restaurant table set up for dinner—no people but with food	0	0	8	0	0	8.3	8.3	0	0	0	8.3	8.3	0	0	8.3	0	0	8.3	41.6	100
Market scene	16.6	0	5.5	11	5.5	0	11.11	0	0	16.6	0	0	5.5	0	0	5.5	0	22.26	0	100
Typical cooked country dishes on their own (tarts, stews)	5.7	7.7	23.6	3.8	0	19	3.8	1.9	0	11.5	7.7	5.7	1.9	0	0	0	3.8	1.9	1.9	100
Typical country products (dried cure ham, olive oil, etc.)	4	4	0	8	0	4	0	0	0	16	0	0	8	12	8	0	4	12	20	100
Cheeses	0	10.7	7.1	3.5	7.1	0	0	3.5	7.1	0	3.5	7.1	10.71	17.8	3.5	0	3.5	10.7	0	100

	R	A	W	P	H	T	G	N	Ar	Ac										
Natural products in their environment (mushrooms in the soil, berries/ fruits/olives on a tree)	9.3	3.1	6.2	0	0	9.4	0	3.1	3.1	9.4	3.1	3.1	9.4	9.4	0	0	21.8	9.4	0	100
Unprepared/raw products (seafood, fruits, etc.)	1.9	5.6	9.4	0	13.2	1.9	0	0	7.5	18.8	0	15.09	0	1.9	0	0	7.5	7.7	7.5	100
Local products (sweets, chocolates)	0	0	0	0	0	38.5	7.7	0	0	7.7	0	0	7.7	0	7.7	0	23	0	0	100
Farmers/ fishermen/ winemaker/ baker/cook	0	3.8	3.8	3.8	15.4	3.8	3.8	7.7	0	3.8	3.8	0	0	3.8	0	0	0	27	15.3	100
Farm animals	33	0	0	9.5	0	0	0	0	4.7	0	9.5	0	4.7	4.7	0	4.7	0	18.5	0	100
Vineyards/ grapes	0	4	12	8	8	0	0	12	0	0	10	2	4	12	0	2	8	16	2	100
Bottle of wine and/or a glass of wine	0	0	15.6	3.1	9.4	0	3.1	0	3.1	3.1	9.4	3.1	3.1	9.4	0	3.1	2.5	3.1	3.1	100
Wine tasting	0	0	0	20	20	0	0	0	0	0	0	0	20	0	0	0	20	20	0	100

R: Rural; A: Authentic; W: Wild; P: Pure; H: History; T: Traditional; G: Gastronomy; N: Natural; Ar: Arts and Crafts; Ac: Activities;

however they do provide an interesting repertory grid to the content analysis and give some indication of the themes used.

The table is analyzed in terms of the categories that received the highest frequency rates. When referring to the rural themes it would appear that market scenes, country dishes and to an extent natural products are more often found among regions that are positioning themselves along the rural/authentic theme. Slight differences can be noted with regions that have positioned themselves on the natural/authentic theme where a higher representation of natural products and unprepared/raw products can be found. The representation of cheeses, local delicacies and images pertaining to wine have to be taken in isolation since they are mostly found in their respective producing areas. For instance, images of cheeses are mostly found in mountainous areas while wine images are to be mainly found in producing areas such as Burgundy, the Loire-valley, Languedoc-Roussillon and Franche Comté although they are not overly represented in Aquitaine where Bordeaux can be found. Overall there does not seem to be major differences between the themes of traditions, rurality and authenticity. Indeed, while the panel separated those positioning themes, similar food images appear to be used to exemplify those three themes. However, the two regions that position themselves on gastronomy (Burgundy and the Riviera) concentrated a higher proportion of restaurant scenes (without people) and food trade. The historical dimension could also be linked to those images since the Region Centre (the Loire Valley) also displays a higher frequency of restaurant style scenes. In the case of burgundy, on top of the restaurant theme, farm animals are overly present, due to its rural identity certainly. Finally, it would seem that the two regions that have positioned themselves on the natural/pure/wild theme (Midi-Pyrénées, Auvergne) do not seem to distinguish themselves clearly from others. This result might be linked to the fact that if regions wish to position themselves on the wild/pure/natural theme they tend to express it through other images than food images. If the natural theme is slightly linked to images of raw/natural food products, it is not the case for wild/pure positioning.

In order to clarify this table, a perceptual map representing the food images and the regions position provided some information (see Graph 1). Mapping was undertaken using the Sphinx software for principal component analysis. The two axes identified explained only 42.9% of the variance, therefore the results will only be used on an exploratory basis.

The number one axis seems to distinguish food production on one side (grouping the food trade and the wine production and cheeses) and food consumption on the other (restaurants/cafés, restaurant tables, production of delicacies). The second axis is more difficult to interpret since it does not distinguish the notions of naturalness and that of countryside/rural foods. Indeed, the second axis groups on one end items pertaining both to natural products and the vast majority of the country produced dishes (apart from cheeses) such as country dishes, country products, markets, cafés, farm animals. This, to some extent, supports the results provided in Table 3: natural and rural food images seem to be easily mixed together to exemplify regions that position themselves on the rural/authentic/traditional themes. However, this second axis has no corresponding theme that can be clearly identified on the other end.

The corresponding regions positioned on this graph indicate that only two regions are clearly identified as food production and rural/traditional areas, that is Burgundy and the Pays de la Loire. On the other side the Cote d'Azur (the Riviera) positions itself strongly on the food service side and indeed this does translate well its positioning strategy of an area of beauty, palaces and to some extent luxury. The other four regions in the upper left quadrant, Lorraine, Nord-Pas-de-Calais, Limousin, Britany, are all characterized as traditional/rural theme and some of them (Britany) have a strong natural/traditional feeling in their positioning. On the contrary, the lower left-hand corner, which is to an extent unspecified, groups regions that are mostly characterized by their naturalness. The other two regions, in the right-hand quadrant, the region Centre and the Aquitaine, have used wine images extensively in their brochures of wine images but this in itself cannot solely explain their location in that quadrant.

DISCUSSION

The study's most important finding lies with its identification of the different types of food images that are used. However, across the 19 regions studied, the general lack of diversity of food pictures is noticeable, i.e., most regions seem to be using similar food themes. What might appear most surprising is the fact that the vast majority of images concerning unprepared, natural products or rural products and their associated rural/countryside lifestyle. In other terms most of the messages portrayed through the images used have an indirect meaning of authenticity and traditions of the French regions. This translates the wish by regions to ascertain their cultural uniqueness but also the authenticity of their assets to attract potential visitors.

GRAPH 1. Positioning of the Regions and Food Images

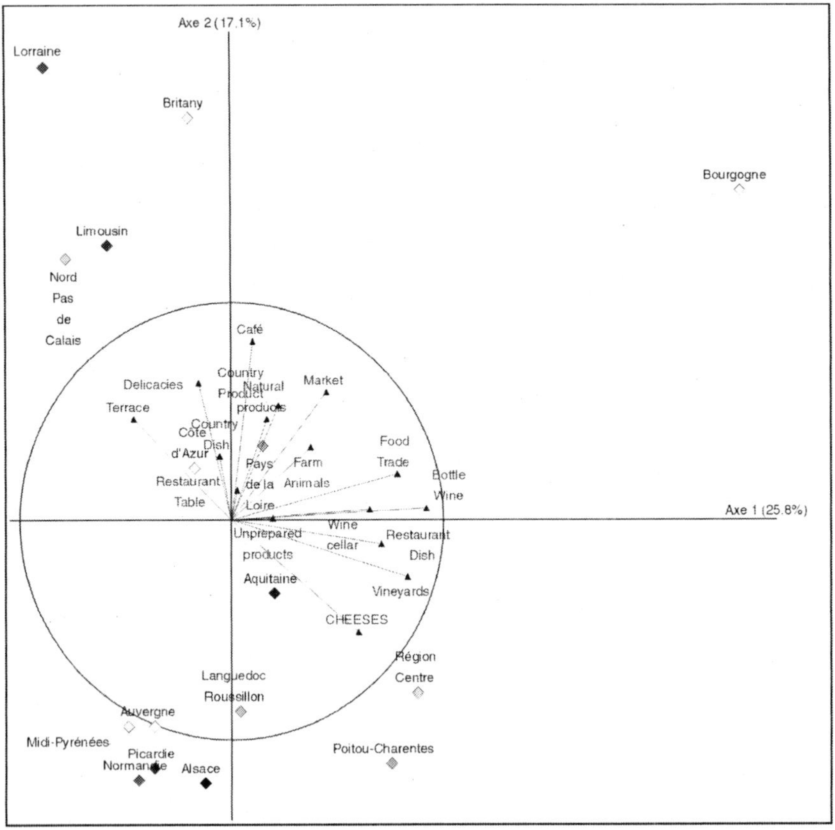

In relation to the sociological meanings of food, it can be clearly identified that food images were most often used to ascertain and strengthen the identity of the regions. Bourdieu (1979) and Poulain (2000) have exemplified the role of food as an identifying and differentiating cultural theme and the present study confirms very strongly this link. The lack of diversity of the food images used to some extent also attests of this fact, i.e., when the food theme is being used in French brochures it is mostly to confirm the uniqueness and authentic culture and traditions of a destination. Nevertheless, beyond that traditional, rural general theme, another theme is important to recognize, that of natural products. Indeed, the trend of the 1990s which saw an increasing consumption of "green" products and an increased consumption from tourists of the outdoors is also present in the brochures. However, if the present study draws a link between natural/raw food images and positioning on the natural theme, this link is rather weak. In fact, overall the analysis does not seem to differentiate regions that use the rural/traditional theme from that of naturalness, in terms of images they seem to be associated and no clear distinctions really seem to exist. Nevertheless, the location of some regions in the bottom left quadrant of the map might indicate some form of commonalities between them but the analysis is not capable of identifying.

Furthermore, the communication theme attached to food consumption (Poulain, 1985) is not overly present in the French regions brochures' images. Apart from market scenes that show images of contacts with local people, very few images of either local peoples or even tourists sharing a meal with or without these local inhabitants can be found. Furthermore, images of food seem to portray either the products or dishes on their own, with no evidence of people. Pictures of restaurant scenes with people, of food producers are also scarce, which is surprising since the image of welcome provided by a region could be associated to a genuine contact with local people (particularly for regions that wish to portray a rural and/or authentic feeling).

Finally, there is in fact very little evidence of food as a status symbol; indeed; images of restaurants and chefs are in fact in a minority across all brochures and are mostly exemplified by two regions, the Riviera and Burgundy. In the Riviera, the image of food chefs, palaces and restaurants is associated to that of "luxury," old and historic sea-side resorts while in Brugundy it is more closely linked to its true rural and traditional dimension and of course to its long term reputation of a land for gastronomes. By far the image of gastronomy, in the sense of renowned chefs and restaurants, is probably the theme least used in the regional brochures.

LIMITATIONS

This study, exploratory by nature, certainly contains some limitations. The fact that regional brochures were used can be a limit since regions are large and can contain in themselves different tourism offerings (e.g., rural tourism, urban tourism seaside resorts) hence this diversity might be a limit to the analysis. For instance, it could be advanced that the variety of the food images used reflect this diversity. Secondly, it is recognized that the analysis is influenced by geographical factors. As was noted, wine, cheese and delicacies are all influenced by geographical factors that make them more present in some regions than others independently from their respective positioning strategies.

Nevertheless, the images reviewed showed that food could indeed be used to portray different strategies. If French brochures use a variety of images, they do not however select carefully those images in relation to their positioning strategies. Indeed, food pictures could be used by those brochures with a closer link to the general image they wish to portray of themselves. The notion of nature and authenticity being popular at present means that those images are heavily used, nevertheless they could be more discerning according to regions' positioning. If French visitors can appreciate the differences between different types of cheeses, wines and some food products it is questionable that foreign visitors can appreciate such differences when reading the brochures. Therefore, if regional tourism organizations use images of specific local products and characteristics, the subtlety of the different images used might bypass foreign visitors' understanding.

CONCLUSION

The present article views food as a potential theme to sharpen destination images and ascertain their uniqueness in comparison to other countries. In this regard France is a good study case since it is renowned for the quality of its gastronomy but also for the uniqueness of its regional cuisine. But more importantly, regional food and cuisine is extremely important and very diversified across France and it has been a tool used by French regions to differentiate themselves on the global market place. However, if the "French uniqueness" is probably not debatable in terms of food traditions, the study of the brochures within France do not show a strong disparity among the regions themselves. Indeed, most regions appear to be using similar food images which concern mostly raw products, products in their environment, countryside dishes and countryside products. Wine and cheeses of course are heavily used but only by regions that are their main producers. Finally, the image of gastronomy, of chefs and of restaurants are not really used apart from two regions identified. In other words, it can be stated that the main message that destinations want to portray is mostly that of their authenticity through images of "real" foods, country traditions and of natural products. Nevertheless, the types of images used in those brochures can certainly be used by other destinations if they wish to achieve a similar positioning; or they might wish to adapt it to their own national/regional positioning. It would be beneficial to undertake further studies, and particularly cross-national studies, to evaluate if the range of food images identified in the present article can be found in other countries but also to identify if food image can be more clearly linked to specific positioning strategies. There is probably scope to ascertain the use of food images in French brochures and link it more strongly to regional positioning strategies, but for this further research is needed.

REFERENCES

Acheson, D. (1990). Food–the vital ingredient. In *Handbook of Tourism*, London: Horwarth and Horwarth, MacMillan Press.

Berger, A.A. (1998). *Media Analysis Techniques*, 2nd Edition, Thousand Oaks: Sage.

Bourdieu, P. (1979). *La distinction Sociale du Jugement,* Paris: Minuit.

Dann, G. (1996). The people of tourist brochures. In T. Selwyn (ed.) *The Tourist Image,* Chichester: Wiley.

Echtner, C.M. & Ritchie, J.R.B. (1993). The measurement of a destination image: An empirical assessment, *Journal of Travel Research*, Spring, 3-13.

Frochot, I.V. (2000). Wine tourism in France, a paradox? In C. M. Hall, L. Sharples, B. Cambourne & N. Macionis (Eds.). *Wine and Tourism From Around the World.* London: Butterworth Heinemann, 67-80.

Frochot, I. & McLellan, R. (2002). Profiling rural tourists: A Scottish perspective, Unpublished Internal paper, The Scottish Hotel School, University of Strathclyde, 36 pages.

Hall C.M. & Mitchell, R. (2000). We are what we eat: Food, tourism and globalization. *Tourism, Culture and Communication*, 2, 29-37.

Hall, C.M., Sharples, L., Cambourne, B. & Macionis, N. (Eds.) (2000). *Wine and Tourism From Around the World.* London: Butterworth Heinemann.

Hjalager, A-M & Corigliano M. A. (2000). Food for tourists–determinants of an image. *International Journal of Tourism Research*, 2, 281-293.

Hu, Y. & Ritchie, J.R.B. (1993). Measuring destination attractiveness: A contextual approach. *Journal of Travel Research*, Fall, 25-34.

Jenkins, O.H. (1999). Understanding and measuring tourist destination images. *International Journal of Tourism Research*, 1, 1-15.

Mellinger, W. (1994). Towards a critical analysis of tourism representations. *Annals of Tourism Research*, 21, 756-779.

Morgan, N. & Pritchard, A. (2000). *Advertising in Tourism and Leisure*, Oxford: Butterworth-Heinemann.

Pearce, P.L. (1982). Perceived changes in holiday destinations. *Annals of Tourism Research*, 9, 145-164.

Poulain, J-P (1996). Pour une anthropo-sociologie de l'alimentation, *Tourismes*, No. 4, Université de Toulouse II.

Poulain, J-P. (2000). Les patrimonies gastronomiques et leurs valorizations touristiques. In Amirou, R. & Bachimon, P. (eds.) *Le Tourisme Local*, Paris: L'Harmattan, 157-235.

Pritchard, A., & Morgan, N.J. (1996). Selling the Celtic arc to the USA: A comparative analysis of the destination brochure images used in the marketing of Ireland, Scotland and Wales, *Journal of Vacation Marketing*, 2(4), 346-365.

Rimmington, M. & Yüksel, A. (1998). Tourist satisfaction and food service experience: Results and implications of an empirical investigation, *Anatolia*, 9(1), 37-57.

Ryan, C. (1997). *The Tourist Experience: the New Introduction*, London: Cassell.

Sancton, T. and Le Quesne, N. (2001, September 10). Some like it haute. *Time*, p. 59-63.

Secrétariat d'Etat au Tourisme (1998). *Le Tourisme International en France*, Paris: Observatoire National du Tourisme.

Smith, L.J.S. (1983). Restaurants and dining out: Geography of a tourism business. *Annals of Tourism Research*, 10, 514-538.

Williams, P. (2001). The evolving images of wine tourism destinations. *Tourism Recreation Research*, 26 (2), 3-10.

The Role of Local and Regional Food
in Destination Marketing:
A South African Situation Analysis

Gerrie E. du Rand
Ernie Heath
Nic Alberts

SUMMARY. An analysis of the relevant tourism literature and the pro-motional material of various destinations indicate that the role of food in the marketing of destinations has until recently received very little atten-tion globally and locally. All indications, however, are that local food holds much potential to enhance sustainability in tourism; contribute to the authenticity of the destination; strengthen the local economy; and provide for the environmentally friendly infrastructure. This paper will highlight the key findings of the preliminary study regarding the utiliza-tion of food as a key or supportive attraction by destination-marketing organizations in South Africa. Guidelines for the future development,

Gerrie E. du Rand is Lecturer, Department of Consumer Science, University of Pre-toria, Pretoria, South Africa, 0002 (E-mail: durandg@postino.up.ac.za). Ernie Heath is Professor and Head, Department of Tourism Management, University of Pretoria, Pre-toria, South Africa, 0002 (E-mail: eheath@orion.up.ac.za). Nic Alberts is Professor, Department of Tourism Management, University of Pretoria, Pretoria, South Africa, 0002 (E-mail: nalberts@orion.up.ac.za).

A Research Grant from Nestlé South Africa supported this research.

[Haworth co-indexing entry note]: "The Role of Local and Regional Food in Destination Marketing: A South African Situation Analysis." du Rand, Gerrie E., Ernie Heath, and Nic Alberts. Co-published simulta-neously in *Journal of Travel & Tourism Marketing* (The Haworth Hospitality Press, an imprint of The Haworth Press, Inc.) Vol. 14, No. 3/4, 2003, pp. 97-112; and: *Wine, Food, and Tourism Marketing* (ed: C. Mi-chael Hall) The Haworth Hospitality Press, an imprint of The Haworth Press, Inc., 2003, pp. 97-112. Single or multiple copies of this article are available for a fee from The Haworth Document Delivery Service [1-800-HAWORTH, 9:00 a.m. - 5:00 p.m. (EST). E-mail address: docdelivery@haworthpress.com].

packaging and marketing of local and regional foods will be postulated and proposals for future research will be outlined. *[Article copies available for a fee from The Haworth Document Delivery Service: 1-800-HAWORTH. E-mail address: <docdelivery@haworthpress.com> Website: <http://www.HaworthPress.com> © 2003 by The Haworth Press, Inc. All rights reserved.]*

KEYWORDS. Food tourism, destination marketing, sustainability

INTRODUCTION

A successful tourism destination is, among others, evaluated by the positive revelations of visitors to the area, the amount of money spent per capita and prospects of repeat visits to the destination. In this regard Murphy, Pritchard and Brock (2000) argue that visitors consume the products of a destination; therefore, the products must be something the visitor wants and needs. A further analysis of the literature indicates that food and drink products of a country can be among its most important cultural expressions (Handszuh, 2000; Bernard & Zaragoza, 1999; Hjalager & Corigliano, 2000). On a practical level a nation's identity is reflected and strengthened by the food experiences that it offers. The way in which various ingredients are combined and cooked forms an important element of a national cultural identity (Bessiere, 1998; Cusack, 2000). Based on these perspectives it can be argued that local and regional food is a feature that can add value to a destination (Telfer & Wall, 1996; Handszuh, 2000), and furthermore may contribute to the sustainable competitiveness of a destination (Crouch & Ritchie, 1999).

The Potential Role of Food Tourism

Until recently, the contribution of food to tourism has been largely ignored in spite of its apparent importance and potential (Telfer & Wall, 1996; Handszuh, 2000; WTO, 2000). So, for example, tourism spending on food and dining out in South Africa by international tourists averages 8% of the total spending (SA Tourism, 2000), while the domestic tourist spends on average 24% (Rule, Struwig, Langa, Viljoen & Boiare, 2001). In light of these figures, it is important to consider the role of food tourism and how it can be utilized and further enhanced to contribute to the effective marketing of a destination. In this regard it is also essential to consider how food tourism can be incorporated in the marketing and promotional material of a region.

Handszuh (2000), argues that local food holds much potential to enhance sustainability in tourism, whereby the tourism planner and the entrepreneur should work hand in hand to satisfy the consumers; contribute to the authenticity of the destination; strengthen the local economy; and provide for the environmentally-friendly infrastructure, including the ways and means by which food resources, both local and imported, are handled. This approach was not always common practice at the local level. Traditionally many local people did not hold their own cuisine in high regard, and often viewed it as not being sophisticated enough and definitely not something a tourist would want (Kapner, 1996). All indications are that this attitude is changing and is in accordance with the market trend where tourists want to experience and "taste" the region they are visiting (Bessiere, 1998; Refalo, 2000), an underlying reason being that culture is playing an increasingly important role in tourism and food is one of the key elements of culture.

Tourists enjoy indigenous food, particularly items of local or ethnic nature (Wagner, 2001). Furthermore knowledge of the local, regional and national cuisine has become an interest for tourists (Chappel, 2001; Gallagher, 2001). Santich (1998), Macdonald (2001) and Bessiere (1998) report that people interested in travelling for gastronomical motivations are on the increase. In spite of these trends, gastronomy has not been considered for its real potential (Bernard & Zaragoza, 1999), nor exploited conveniently as a tourism resource. It needs to be identified and applied as a branding mechanism for a destination. For emerging destinations such as South Africa to compete with the other leading destinations and meet or improve on their food tourism initiatives, it is important to learn from existing best practices and then benchmark the country's initiatives against global best practices (Wolf, 2002; Hall et al., 2003).

From the preceding perspectives it is apparent that food tourism has considerable potential to enhance visitor experiences and to contribute to the branding and competitive marketing of destinations. It is, however, important to insure that the authentic cuisine of a region and marketable local and regional foods are approached with a delicate balance. If food is changed only to suit the taste of foreign tourists, then traditional foods of the region can be lost, which has wider implications regarding the sustainability of the community (Chappel, 2001).

Focussing on the Role of Local Food

As governments in developing countries increasingly embrace international tourism, they should not underestimate the importance of food service as a vital part of their overall development and marketing strategies (Elmont, 1995). The use of local food can directly or indirectly contribute to the various elements of sustainability in a particular area (see Figure 1), namely stimulating and supporting agricultural activity and food production; preventing authentic exploitation; enhancing destination attractiveness; empowerment of the community (by means of job creation and encouraging entrepreneurship); generating pride, specifically regarding food; and reinforcing brand identity of the destination with the focus on food experiences in that area (Telfer & Wall, 1996). Furthermore, food service is a generator of jobs and income that is of major importance to the tourism sector in these countries, including South Africa, and can contribute to the establishment of a destination that is both sustainable and competitive (Elmont, 1995).

FIGURE 1. The Contribution of Local Food to Sustainable Development Within a Destination

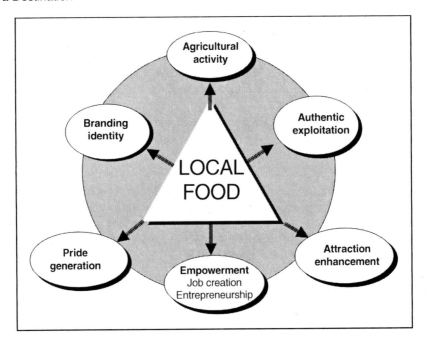

The reality regarding food tourism is that local food in the form of regional cuisine is rarely present as an important resource in publicity material and promotional messages prepared for mainstream tourism (Handszuh, 2000). This also appears to be the case in South Africa and therefore it has become essential to explore opportunities to promote food tourism and more specifically its culinary heritage. The popular perception that food is regarded as a given (as tourists need to eat), relative to other attractions, needs to be challenged. A key question that needs to be answered is if local and regional food does not hold a sufficiently strong appeal to attract visitors and can it not be elevated to a key attraction in many destinations with considerable untapped potential?

When developing the food potential of a particular area the warning should be heeded to, that the presence of tourists might negatively impact the local culture. Appropriate planning and coordination is therefore essential to prevent the altering of social values and diminishing standards concerning food production (Handszuh, 2000; Nield, Kozak and LeGrys, 2000). Care must therefore be taken to assure that definite checks and balances are in place to prevent exploitation of the local community and environment, thereby assuring the sustainability of food tourism as not purely an income generating activity but also as a cultural enhancement activity and eminently contributing to the sustainability of the destination.

OBJECTIVES OF THE STUDY

Against the background of the preceding perspectives the objectives of this preliminary study were to determine the following regarding food tourism in South Africa:

- the current status of food as an attraction in destinations;
- the current role of food in destination marketing strategies;
- the constraints and gaps experienced in utilizing local and regional food as attractions and as key elements of destination marketing strategies;
- guidelines for future strategy development; and
- key recommendations for future research.

METHODOLOGY AND DATA ANALYSIS

To address the above objectives a survey was conducted at INDABA (2001), the annual South African tourism-marketing exhibition, which is attended by leading Southern Africa destination and product marketers and key overseas tour operators. A convenience sampling method was applied in accordance with specific criteria. Only target groups representing key substructure agents in food/culinary tourism and agents of tourism, namely the Destination Marketing Organizations (DMOs) in South Africa, were included in the study. To be included in the sample the organization had to comply to the following criteria, namely be a:

- South African Provincial, Regional or Local DMO, or
- South African key marketer/organisation in food/culinary tourism.

A sample of 80 South African local, regional and provincial destination-marketing organizations and other marketers complying with the criteria were selected. Information was collected by means of a structured questionnaire consisting primarily of close-ended questions. Open-ended questions were also included to accommodate answers that did not fall into specific categories. The questions covered information regarding the attractions of the particular destination; the role of food as a key or supportive attraction; marketing tools and activities applied by destination marketing organisations; marketing constraints and gaps and possible strategies that can be applied to market the food experiences of a destination.

Of the 80 questionnaires distributed, 58 were returned and were considered suitable for analysis. Frequency ratings expressed as percentages were calculated regarding the status of an attraction; the role of food as a key or supportive attraction; and the key constraints, possible strategies and recommendations. The responses are reported reflecting the categories of each question in the questionnaire. The responses of the open-ended questions were listed and grouped together according to meaningful categories. Due to multiple responses for questions concerning information reflected in Tables 1 through 6 the percentages reflect the number of responses for each category indicated by the respondents and not the number of respondents.

FINDINGS AND DISCUSSION

The key findings of the preliminary study as stated in the objectives of the study are outlined below:

TABLE 1. Key Components of Food Tourism

KEY COMPONENTS OF FOOD TOURISM	n = 42* %
Speciality restaurants/eating places	62
Locally/regionally produced food products	59
Special cuisine/food routes	45
Food festivals	31
Special food events	19
Other	14

*(n = 42) number of respondents that indicated food as a key/supportive attraction.

TABLE 2. Nature of Food Experiences Offered

NATURE OF FOOD EXPERIENCES OFFERED	n = 30* %
Speciality restaurant/eating place promotion	63
Food festivals	47
Included in locally produced food product promotions	37
Special food promotional events	33

*(n = 30) number of respondents that indicated that local/regional food is used as a marketing tool/activity.

TABLE 3. Communication Tools Used in Food Marketing

COMMUNICATION TOOLS USED IN FOOD MARKETING	n = 30* %
Included in marketing tools/brochures/pamphlets	80
Included in advertising initiatives/radio/TV/media/printed material/advertising/publicity	63
A key element of the image/branding identity	60
Included in trade/consumer exhibitions/shows	57
Included in web promotion	53
Other	13

*(n = 30) number of respondents that indicated that local/regional food is used as a marketing tool/activity.

The Current Status of Food as an Attraction in Destinations

In a destination such as South Africa, nature-based attractions are the most important key attractions followed by cultural and outdoor and recreational activities. The focus of this study, however, was to deter-

TABLE 4. Promotional Gaps/Constraints of Food Promotion in a Destination

PROMOTIONAL GAPS/CONSTRAINTS OF FOOD PROMOTION IN A DESTINATION	n = 39* %
Insufficient funds available to develop and promote the food experience	74
No special food events are organized	61
In spite of our potential food is not promoted as a special tourist attraction	59
Food is not included in any media coverage of the destination	54
Food does not feature in any of the brochures/pamphlets of the destination	49
No speciality restaurants/eating places that offer local/regional foods	46
No regional branding of locally produced food products	41
No locally produced food products are exported	41
Other	31

*(n = 39) number of respondents indicating that there are gaps/constraints in the promotion of food in a destination.

TABLE 5. Initiatives Required to Address Gaps/Constraints in Food Promotion

INITIATIVES REQUIRED TO ADDRESS GAPS/CONSTRAINTS IN FOOD PROMOTION	n = 39* %
Marketing strategy/initiatives/procedures	36
Branding/promotion of local products/menus reflecting local food	20
Promotional material required/advertisements	18
Development of a culinary route/addition to wine route	15
Organisation of food festivals/food promotion/exhibitions	13
Sponsors/funding	10
Training to staff of DMOs and educating providers	10
Tourism policy incorporation of food tourism/sustainability of local food	10
Package food together with other key attractions in destination	5
Improve foodservice standards and quality	5

**(n = 39) number of respondents indicating that there are gaps/constraints in the promotion of food in a destination.

mine where food would be positioned. Figure 2 portrays a very positive image where food was indicated by 32.7% of the destination marketing organizations as a key attraction and by 39.7% destination marketing organizations as a supportive attraction, making food the prime supportive attraction. Wine in comparison was only indicated by 13.8% of destination marketing organizations as a key attraction. The majority of destinations where food was a key attraction were in the Cape Province,

TABLE 6. Possible Strategies That Can Contribute to Optimising a Destination's Potential

POSSIBLE STRATEGIES THAT CAN CONTRIBUTE TO OPTIMISING A DESTINATION'S POTENTIAL (n = 58)	Major importance %	Limited importance %	No importance %
Media coverage of all local/regional foods	64	17	2
Sufficient funds available to develop and promote the food experience	60	19	2
Promotion of speciality restaurants/eating places	60	20	3
Development of local/regional food as a special tourist attraction of the destination	55	19	2
Branding/marketing of locally produced food products	55	17	3
Brochures/pamphlets accentuating role of local/regional foods	55	21	2
Launching of a regional food festival	48	24	10
Exporting of local food products	45	21	9
Trade/consumer exhibitions/shows	40	33	7
Development of a special food/wine tourist route	34	28	10
Organizing of special food events	28	31	7

followed by Gauteng. A possible reason for this could be the existing wine routes in the Western Cape, which have fostered the development of food tourism in that area. Gauteng, which includes Soweto and various other cultural villages, has promoted the culinary heritage of the African culture and promoted it as an authentic tourist experience in this area. Food as a supportive attraction was more evenly represented in all the various provinces of South Africa. This finding supports the fact that food is a product that is provided in all destinations. DMOs, however, can promote the food of a destination with potential and move it from being a supportive attraction to enhancing it in becoming a key attraction.

The key components of food tourism, as reflected in Table 1, lie strongly in the presence of specialty restaurants and the local or regionally produced food products of the area. This is in accordance with expectations as this is the traditional way of showcasing the food of a region and offering the tourist a cultural experience. Of particular significance is the finding that routes, festivals and events are also receiving considerable attention.

FIGURE 2. Relative Position of Food as an Attraction

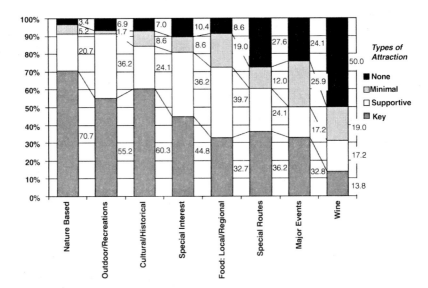

The Current Role of Food in Destination Marketing Strategies

The traditional way that food experiences are offered in a destination is reflected by the promotion of restaurants (Table 2). This form of food experience occurs more easily as food has to be provided to tourists, it does not involve additional effort, organisation and promotional activities as for example a food festival would require.

Fifty-two percent of the respondents (n = 58) indicated that food is used as a marketing activity or tool in promoting the destination.

The communication tools used in food marketing reflected the use of the traditional methods of marketing communication as indicated in Table 3. Although these tools are the most generally utilized by most DMOs the information regarding food tourism in the pamphlets, brochures and media advertisements evaluated is scant; not informative enough; and often primarily in the form of advertisements, where the provider is advertised and not necessarily the generic food products of the region. Very little information is provided with regards to the culinary heritage or the authentic food tourism experience of the region. Of significance is the finding that a considerable percentage of respondents use food as a key element of their branding identity and also include it in their web promotion.

The Perceived Constraints and Gaps Regarding Food Tourism

The perceived constraints and gaps are outlined in Table 4. Insufficient funding appears to be the major problem encountered by many of the DMOs concerning the promotion of food in a destination. When funds are insufficient, the promotion of food, which is considered a product that will be consumed regardless whether it is promoted or not, will not be included in the marketing efforts. The additional gaps and constraints hampering food promotion concern the specific marketing strategies, promotional initiatives and activities of the destination. This is a more challenging problem to solve as it involves the DMOs making a mind shift regarding the importance of local food in destination marketing.

Table 5 provides respondents' views on initiatives required to address the perceived gaps and constraints. More than a third (36%) of all the respondents that indicated the need for promotional tools specified that marketing strategies were required as an initiative to promote food tourism in a destination. The other responses strengthen this recommendation, as food tourism is not considered essential in the planning and marketing actions of a DMO.

Guidelines for Future Strategy Development

The possible strategies and recommendations made regarding optimising a destinations' potential and the use of food to enhance a destination are outlined in Table 6. Aside from funding that is required for all types of promotional incentives in a destination, the strategies that can contribute the most to optimising a destinations' potential with regard to food tourism are all promotion and market orientated (Table 6). The providers of food services and the products of the area need to be boosted and branded as the local and specialty products of that area. Specific recommendations that require a concerted effort from all stakeholders in a destination are the following:

- Creation of "proud of local food."
- Development of an identification system for locally produced food/branding identity/packaging identity.
- Empowerment of local SMMEs to establish food services utilizing locally produced foods.

A recommendation that could provide a positive development would be the development of food routes in various regions, that would not involve much additional effort or funding as many areas are already developing different cultural/scenic routes and food could easily be included as part of the marketing strategy.

CONCLUSION AND RECOMMENDATIONS FOR FURTHER RESEARCH

Food as an Attraction in Destinations

Food does play a role in tourism, and is primarily considered as a supportive attraction and, to a lesser extent, a key attraction in South Africa. Tourism spending on food and dining out in South Africa by international tourists (8%) and domestic tourists (24%) is substantial enough to warrant more aggressive marketing as a form of niche tourism. It could contribute to the promotion of food tourism in destinations that have the resources (local food products/suitable providers) but that are not exploiting their potential related to food tourism.

When analysing the reasons where food is not promoted as a key or supportive attraction it can be concluded that there are certain financial and marketing restraints or lack of knowledge regarding local and regional food. Marketing efforts regarding food tourism are lacking not only in South Africa but also globally (Handszuh, 2000) and are an issue that can be addressed if DMOs start to develop strategies to incorporate food as part of their overall marketing strategies. To enable the DMOs to achieve this goal a tool needs to be developed which will assist them. This is one of the envisaged key outcomes of this study, namely the development of a product potential and attractiveness audit instrument that will contribute to providing a framework and guidelines to destination marketers and current and prospective entrepreneurs, to optimise the tourism potential of local and regional foods in future destination marketing.

Role of Food in Destination Marketing Strategies

The marketing strategies and tools that were identified as being used by the various DMOs constituted a wide spectrum, but only 52% of the total sample indicated that they used these tools. The reality is that nearly half of the DMOs are not applying any specific strategies to promote food tourism, which clearly underlines the need for a product potential and attractiveness audit instrument, appropriate guidelines and a framework to enable DMOs to put in a more concerted effort regarding the marketing and promotion of food tourism.

The necessary actions that have been identified to promote and develop food tourism offer a great challenge to DMOs. The actions entail both policy and strategy development actions and specific products or services that can be developed. The recommended strategies as identified by the DMOs entail formulation of policy and the marketing and promotion of tourism products and services within a destination, such as development of promotional material and branding the products of a destination. The development of a strategy and the application of a policy are activities that can be streamlined by applying a tool, guidelines and developing a framework that can assist the DMOs in formulating a food tourism strategy. Specific product and service development would require the necessary resources that would include knowledge of the local and regional food products and experiences, to facilitate the development of food tourism in a destination.

Guidelines for Future Strategy Development

Strategy development, packaging and marketing of local and regional food entail the development and marketing of appropriate products and experiences, but more importantly the implementation of these initiatives by DMOs.

The following are suggestions that can be considered by the DMOs:

- Be sensitive to local conditions–use local foods instead of imported foods.
- Enhance domestic tourism as standards of living improve.
- An attractive/unusual/unknown cuisine can be regarded as a resource of a destination and needs to be developed as a destination branding item.
- Gastronomy routes can promote a destination and can contribute to sustainable tourism projects.
- Specialty restaurants can be developed to assist with the promotion of the special cuisine of an area.

A key question is: How can food tourism in South Africa be marketed successfully? In this regard certain suggestions made by Bannister (2001) pertaining to the promotion of tourism to South Africa can also be applied to local and regional food tourism. These include the following:

- Maintain a public relations and media management campaign to keep a unique destination profile of a combination of authentic experiences and a sophisticated infrastructure. This is where food tourism can find a definite place as it can be marketed for its exotic and authentic experience.
- Create a visual experience either by developing virtual "food" tourism and promoting food tourism in the "Project Hollywood" which is being negotiated by SA Tourism and deserves the support from government and international marketing organisations.
- Continue with campaigns such as "Circle of Sunshine" and "Celebrate South Africa" but include the rich and authentic resources of food and culinary heritage in these promotional efforts.
- Focus on tourists and lure them into coming to SA for the real experience by promoting the key attractions and also focussing on the secondary attractions such as food tourism.
- Local governments should encourage tourism, including the development of food service businesses, to boost the economy and create jobs and contribute to the development of a sustainable destination.

The increase in tourism volume and a more discerning clientele has spurred the more alert of South Africa's entrepreneurs and the more innovative and adventurous chefs to invest in the development of local cuisine. The challenge is for this to develop without losing any of the cuisines' fragrance, taste and originality and preventing it from becoming a fusion of confused tastes and flavors with no definite distinction of the various cultures of our country.

Possibly the key challenge regarding development of food tourism in South Africa is the utilisation of local food as a catalyst for local pride. South Africans need to cultivate a pride in that which is their own and realise the advantages of promoting their local and regional cuisine and culinary heritage.

Proposals for Future Research

This preliminary study has indicated that food tourism in South Africa has not capitalised on this ideal opportunity to promote each local tourism region for what it excels in as far as food is concerned. Future research is required to determine the culinary heritage of each tourism area in terms of local and regional cuisine. It is also imperative to identify the local food produced in each area, region and province, thereby incorporating it into the local cuisine and promoting the products according to region and locality, which can contribute to sustainability in such an area.

When the data of this preliminary study was analysed it was found that the destinations regarding food as a key and supportive attraction were represented from the entire country and not only a specific region, as was the case with the wine. This poses a greater challenge for further study as it will be imperative to identify the regions which are more prone to food tourism and that have a greater chance of promoting and marketing the local and regional food of the region more successfully. Much of this information is either available on ENPAT (Environmental Potential Atlas) or can be added to the existing ENPAT database and assist in providing additional data concerning the tourist (consumer) and the tourism product (food experience) in the various tourism regions.

The development of a product potential and attractiveness audit instrument that will provide a framework and guidelines to destination marketers and current and prospective entrepreneurs, to optimise the tourism potential of local and regional foods in future destination marketing is one of the envisaged key outcomes of the longer term research project concerning food tourism in South Africa. This instrument that together with the data from ENPAT may be utilized by DMOs during strategy formulation and implementation and provide information and guidelines to providers of food products and services in a destination and contribute to the development of food tourism in a destination.

REFERENCES

Bannister, P. (2001, September 23). US disaster presents tourism opportunity–if we're snappy. *Sunday Times*, Business Section.

Bernard, A., & Zaragoza, I. (1999, May). *Art And Gastronomy Routes: An Unexplored Tourism Proposal for Latin America*. Paper presented at the First Pan-American Conference.

Bessiere, J. (1998). Local development and heritage: Traditional food and cuisine as tourist attractions in rural areas. *Sociologia Ruralis*, 38 (1), 21-34.

Chappel, S (2001). *Globalization and Gastronomic Tourism*. Abstract retrieved 9/21/2001, from CAE Globalization Project, [On-line] Available: *http://business. unisa.edu.au/cae/globalization/abstracts.htm*

Crouch, G.I., & Ritchie, J.R.B. (1999). Tourism, competitiveness and social prosperity. *Journal of Business Research*, 44, 137-152.

Cusack, I. (2000). African Cuisines: Recipes for Nation Building? *Journal of African Cultural Studies*, 13 (2), 207-225.

Elmont, S. (1995). Tourism and food service. Two sides of the same coin. *Cornell Hotel and Restaurant Administration Quarterly*, February, 57-63.

Gallagher, B. (2001, October). *The Role of Food and Beverage in Tourism*. Keynote address presented at the Tourism as a Catalyst for Community Development Conference, Pretoria.

Hall, C.M., Sharples, E., Mitchell, R., Cambourne, B., & Macionis, N. (eds.) (2003). *Food Tourism Around the World: Development, Management and Markets*, Oxford: Butterworth-Heinemann.

Handszuh, H. (2000, November). *Local Food in Tourism Policies*. Paper presented at the International Conference on Local Food and Tourism, Larnaka, Cyprus.

Hjalager, A., & Corigliano, M.A. (2000). Food for tourists-determinants of an image. *International Journal of Tourism Research*, 2, 281-293.

Kapner, S. (1996). Caribbean hotel chefs seek to elevate local fare over "continental" imports. *National Restaurant News*, November 11, 49-50.

Macdonald, H.S. (2001). *National Tourism and Cuisine Forum: "Recipes For Success."* (Proceedings and Final Report). Ottawa: Canadian Tourism Commission.

Murphy, P., Pritchard, M.P., & Smith, B. (2000). The destination product and its impact on traveller perceptions. *Tourism Management*, 21(1), 43-52.

Nield, K., Kozak, M., & LeGrys, G. (2000). The role of food service in tourist satisfaction. *Hospitality Management*, 19, 375-384.

Refalo, M. (2000). *Address on the Occasion of the Cookery and Food Review Launch*. (Press Release No. 0988). Malta: Department of Information.

Rule, S., Struwig, J., Langa, Z., Viljoen, J., & Boiare, O. (2001). *South African Domestic Tourism Survey: Marketing the Provinces*. HSRC and DEAT.

Santich, B. (1999, 22 June). Location, location, location. *The Age*. [On-line] Available: *http://www.theage.com.au/daily/990622/food/food.1.html*

SA Tourism [On-line]. Available: *http://www.southafricantourism.com/tourismactionplan/index.html*

Telfer, D. & Wall, G. (1996). Linkages Between Tourism and Food Production. *Annals of Tourism Research*, 23(3), 635-653.

Wagner, H.A. (2001). Marrying food and travel . . . culinary tourism. *Canada's Food News, Foodservice Insights*.

World Tourism Organization Secretariat (2000). *Local Food in Tourism Policies*. [On-line]. Available: *http://www.world-tourism.org/quality@world-tourism.org*

Wolf, E. (2002). *Culinary Tourism: A Tasty Economic Proposition*. Portland: International Culinary Tourism Taskforce.

Wine and Tourism at the "Fairest Cape": Post-Apartheid Trends in the Western Cape Province and Stellenbosch (South Africa)

Imre Josef Demhardt

SUMMARY. The paper gives a background on viticulture and wine making in South Africa before outlining post-apartheid developments in the supply and demand side of the wine industry. Against a sketch of recent tourism patterns in the Western Cape Province and especially the Winelands the linkage between wine and tourism is investigated by a closer look to the South African wine capital Stellenbosch and the Stellenbosch Wine Route. A new trend in wine tourism is highlighted by a case study of the hybrid wine and tourism developments at Spier Resort. *[Article copies available for a fee from The Haworth Document Delivery Service: 1-800-HAWORTH. E-mail address: <docdelivery@haworthpress.com> Website: <http://www.HaworthPress.com> © 2003 by The Haworth Press, Inc. All rights reserved.]*

KEYWORDS. South Africa, Western Cape Province, wine industry, wine tourism, Stellenbosch, Spier Resort

Imre Josef Demhardt can be reached at Otto-Witte-Str. 40, 65197 Wiesbaden, Germany (E-mail: demhardt@geographie.tu-darmstadt.de).

[Haworth co-indexing entry note]: "Wine and Tourism at the 'Fairest Cape': Post-Apartheid Trends in the Western Cape Province and Stellenbosch (South Africa)." Demhardt, Imre Josef. Co-published simultaneously in *Journal of Travel & Tourism Marketing* (The Haworth Hospitality Press, an imprint of The Haworth Press, Inc.) Vol. 14, No. 3/4, 2003, pp. 113-130; and: *Wine, Food, and Tourism Marketing* (ed: C. Michael Hall) The Haworth Hospitality Press, an imprint of The Haworth Press, Inc., 2003, pp. 113-130. Single or multiple copies of this article are available for a fee from The Haworth Document Delivery Service [1-800-HAWORTH, 9:00 a.m. - 5:00 p.m. (EST). E-mail address: docdelivery@haworthpress.com].

On 2 February 1659 Jan van Riebeeck, who on behalf of the Dutch East India Company founded the victual station at the Table Bay in 1652, noted in his diary: "Today, praise be the Lord, wine was made for the first time from Cape grapes." Although these first drops from French roots are said to have been of rather inferior quality viticulture at the Cape–to Sir Francis Drake and most of today's visitors "the fairest Cape in the whole world"–proved to be an immediate success due to the demand by the ship crews calling at Table Bay (Bulpin, 1994). However, the decisive boost to the infant South African wine industry was the advent of a few hundred Huguenot refugees in 1688 who were settled by the Dutch East India Company in the present-day Winelands bringing along from their ungracious country of birth new varieties and the state of the art know how of wine-making. Many of the wine estates here proudly trace back their tradition to the vineyards and homesteads founded by Calvinist refugees and several of their early varieties are cultivated still today (Bulpin, 1994). The first to reach fame was the Muscat which enjoyed popularity overseas throughout the eighteenth and nineteenth centuries. Winemakers at the Cape are still proud that the last sip of wine Napoleon asked for on St. Helena Island shortly before his death had been a Cape Muscadel.

Today the culture and industries around the Cape viticulture has developed into the fourth most important South African tourism attraction and the national prime rural attraction to overseas visitors far ahead of the national "trademark" nature reserves and game sanctuaries. At the same time the booming South African wine industry increasingly depends on leisure and tourist visitors to sustain the growth of local and export sales both as regard to immediate turnover by "over the counter" sales and long term image creating factor. This paper therefore aims to provide a survey of structures and recent trends in wine and tourism development at the Cape and some aspects of their interrelation.

VINEYARDS–
THE GOLD FIELDS OF THE WESTERN CAPE PROVINCE

The vineyards in South Africa traditionally were limited to the small coastal stretch in the south western corner of the Cape between the shores of the Atlantic and Indian Oceans and the Cape mountain ranges being blessed–in a sharp contrast to the rest of South Africa–with moderate temperatures and sufficient precipitation due to a Mediterranean style winter rainfall climate. Only the introduction of large scale irrigation schemes since the Second World War extended the vineyards beyond this natural inward limit. Along the hot and dry valley of the Orange River the only major wine region outside the Western Cape Province's winter rainfall area developed with about a tenth of the national hectarage but specialised in dried sultanas with only few white and red wines. Today more than 90% of the vineyards and the associated wine industry are concentrated in the Western Cape comprising only about a tenth of the South African territory.

In terms of labor the wine industry in 1999 directly employed about 96,000 people and supported about 216,000 people throughout the economy of which about two-thirds could be found in the Western Cape. It is estimated that in this province about 11% or 23,000 people are employed in the broad field of wine related tourism (SAWID, 2000). While almost half of the province's 9,700 commercial farms today engage at least partially in the production of wine and table grapes, throughout the 1980s and 1990s the vineyards held about a quarter of the agricultural land in the province. Due to diverging topography and climate the wine industry at the Cape has two locations: In the narrow stretch between the oceans shores and the mountain ranges with sufficient natural precipitation the vineyards concentrate on the production of good wine, while in the hot and dry valleys and basins in the mountain ranges with intensive artificial irrigation growers focus on the production of desert wines and table grapes (Cape of Good Hope Bank/ WESGRO, 1999; WESGRO, 2001; Wiese, 1999; SAWID, 2000).

In 1973 the legislation recognized a comprehensive system of quality control by introducing the "wines of origin"-scheme which finally brought the South African wine industry in line with European regulations (SAWID, 2000). This ensured a strict control from the crushing of the grapes to the final product with respect to the certification of (various forms of) origin, variety and vintage. Subsequently the wine growing areas have been classified by five regions which were broken into fourteen smaller districts, numerous wards with specific meso-climates and terroirs and finally individual estates. The production of wine of origin soared from about 65 million litres or only 19% of the total wine production in 1994 to 180 million litres or 37% in 2000. But the share of the estates–until the turn of the Millennium almost hundred estates have been identified in terms of the wine of origin-scheme with only five so far opting for de-registration since–in this top end of the market segment stagnated in recent years around 14 million litres (SAWID, 2000; SAWIS, 2001).

To stimulate the desire for high quality wines the South African National Wine Show Association was founded in 1977 to present the South African Young Wine Show and the nowadays top accolade, the Veritas Award, was instigated in 1991 (SAWID, 2000). In line with international consumer preferences in the 1990s the South African vineyards once predominantly planted with white varieties saw more than a doubling of the red varieties from 15.4% in 1990 to 32.0% in 2000. At the dawn of the Millennium almost three quarters of all new plantings were red varieties. While the traditional white bulk variety Chenin Blanc was the main loser–although still occupying 21% in all vineyards–the only shining star on the white side due to increased local and overseas demand was the dry and often barrique-wooded Chardonnay which more than tripled its share to 5%. The red varieties too saw some twists along their increasingly successful inroads into the markets with the former red bulk variety Hermitage diminished while Cabernet Sauvignon and Pinotage–a South African crossing of Pinot Noir and Hermitage–today make up for half of red varieties (SAWIS, 2001).

In 2000 the South African wine industry comprised a total of 4,501 primary grape producers with 105,566 hectares of vineyards–an increase by 13% from the 93,281 ha planted in 1989–and the majority producing less than 100 tons of grapes per annum. But only 355 cellars crushed the grapes and matured the juice, among them 69 co-operatives, 92 recognized estate wine cellars, 185 non-estate wine cellars and 9 producing wholesalers. As with the grape producers the majority of the 277 estate and non-estate private wine cellars are rather small: 106 handle only up to 100 tons and 93 up to 500 tons of crushed grapes. The total replacement worth of the investments in the wine industry was estimated to be just short of R 12.9 billions[1] with about 350,000 people including dependents (SAWIS 2001) representing about 0.8% of all South Africans making their living from the vineyards and cellars. In 1998 the total turnover of the South African wine industry amounted to R 6,988 millions and R 792 millions or 11% were achieved by direct exports. If one compares the South African wine industry with other countries of production and consumption in 1998 its vineyards hectarage ranged sixteenth, way behind the leading countries Spain (1,180,000 ha), France (914,000 ha) and Italy (899,000 ha). But its wine production of 815.6 million litres secured South Africa seventh rank behind the leading countries Italy (5.42 billion litres), France (5.27 billion litres) and Spain (3.03 billion litres). Due to the concentration of the wine industry in the Western Cape about two-thirds of its contribution to the national Gross Domestic Product (GDP) of R 11.7 billions has a direct impact on this province's macro economy with a value of about a tenth of the provincial GDP. About R 2.1 billions or 18% of the national turnover can be attributed to wine tourism activities (SAWID, 2000; SAWIS, 2001).

Looking at the domestic market over the last two decades the consumption of wine and its derivatives have had mixed fortunes. While the total consumption increased–but less than the increase of population–from 330.9 million litres in 1986 by 17% to 388.8 million liters in 2000, the consumption of fortified wines has halved since the 1980s with only 27.3 million litres sold in 2000. As to the per capita consumption of wine in 1999 South Africa ranked thirtieth in global terms with just short of nine litres way behind France with 57.2 litres and the highest per capita consumer, Luxembourg, with 61.0 litres (SAWIS, 2001). In total the domestic market in 2000 took about 404.5 million litres of wine and derivatives with wine making up for 356.6 million litres or 88% while fortified wines (27.27 billion litres), brandy (15.68 billion litres) and sparkling wines (4.99 billion litres) shared in the rest. By far the highest prices were reached by the noble red varieties (Cabernet Sauvignon, Merlot, Shiraz, Pinotage and Pinot Noir) which in 2000 for bulk wine were worth R 7.45 per litre or almost four times the average price per litre of wine (SAWIS, 2001).

The apartheid South Africa's *haute-gout* and associated sanctions hampered both the wine export and the influx of overseas tourists during the first half of the 1990s. However, immediate marketing efforts of the wine industry on strategic overseas markets prompted wine exports to triple between 1993 and 1995. Spurred further by an increase in the domestic wine consumption substantial investments were made throughout the wine industry which experienced a gold rush-like expansion in the second half of the 1990s. In 1999 alone about 40 new wine farms or estates and about 500 new wine labels hit the market (WESGRO, 2001: 1). Exports soared from only 50.7 million litres (12%) in 1994 up to 139.5 million litres (26%) in 2000. Of this most recent figure not less than 99.2% is still wine, with 0.5% sparkling wine and 0.3% fortified wine. Looking only to the still wine sector the single most important export market for South Africa by far is the United Kingdom which in 2000 took up 42% of the total bottled and bulk exports, followed by the rapidly growing "emerging" markets the Netherlands (18%), Scandinavia (9%) and Germany (8%) coinciding well with the fact that these are the main overseas tourism markets for South Africa. While there is still a lot of potential to increase exports to European markets the US market remained still almost untouched with only 2.1 million litres or 1.5% of the exports (SAWIS 2001).

The conclusion of the free trade agreement between South Africa and the European Union in 2000 has triggered a far flung restructuring of both the domestic and overseas marketing especially of the wine derivatives. France, Spain, Portugal and Italy made it a *conditio sine qua non* for allowing South Africa preferential access to the European markets that the Cape's "imitations" of their nationally protected brands as Champagne, Sherry, Port or Grappa are phased out from the South African wine labels although in some cases they were in use for decades. Given transition periods of up to ten years the South African wine industry currently is looking around for new names to re-position well established products like the Cape Port on domestic and overseas markets.

SKETCHING TOURISM PATTERNS: THE WINELANDS AND ITS HUB STELLENBOSCH

The importance of the booming tourism economy for the South African GDP is demonstrated by its rise within the last decade from 4.5% (1991) to 6.4% (1999), outperforming by far all other sectors of the economy. While the traditional (white) domestic tourism still outnumbers overseas (European) tourism an average member of the latter segment spends about five times as much as a local during a vacation trip. Surveys of both domestic and overseas tourists indicate that the wine routes of the Western Cape are by far the most visited non-urban tourism attractions of South Africa (Demhardt, 2000, 2003) with the most popular one being the Stellenbosch Wine Route housing the most nationally as internationally well established trademark estates and cellars in the province.

The core area of viticulture and wine tourism in the Cape are the so-called Winelands occupying the fertile farmlands between the metropolitan area of Cape Town and the Cape mountain ranges with the traditional hubs Franschhoek, Paarl and most prominently Stellenbosch. The latter town was founded as second oldest of the European settlements at the Cape in 1679. Amidst a rolling and fertile natural landscape transformed over more than three centuries into a "romantic" cultural landscape afoot a mountain range it grew to become an economic and educational centre with the oldest South African university (1918)–today the only national institution for study in viticulture and oenology. As a result of its long history the town boasts about one hundred national monuments along its oak lined streets, the biggest concentration in the country, well preserved and complemented by several museums and all tourist amenities. Due to its tranquil agricultural setting but yet close to the centre of Cape Town being only 40 km to the west, Stellenbosch in recent years grew rapidly to about 75,000 inhabitants. They are employed by a well diversified economy based on a services, research and development poll within the greater Cape Town area and the agro-industry focused on wine. Being one of the most sought-after residential areas in the province Stellenbosch strives to stem the urban sprawl from the Cape Town suburbs, which has encroached the farmlands already being as close as 15 km, and threatening already several times the municipal independence which is presently maintained by rural land use and supporting viticulture which acts as a sort of *cordon sanitaire.*

The latest available economic impact study of tourism in the Stellenbosch district estimated that in 1997 all direct spending amounted to R 843 millions of which almost equal shares were derived from overnight visitors and day visitors. The contribution of the almost entirely day visiting business at the wine enterprises around the town was estimated to reach R 148 millions or 18% of the municipal direct tourism turn-over. The employment of the tourism industries with wine tourism being the single most important factor was estimated at 10,800 and of the whole tourism economy at 12,400 (Leibold & Steyn, 1998) representing more than about a quarter of all permanent and seasonal jobs.

According to a survey of the domestic tourism in the Western Cape in 1999 almost two-thirds (65%) of the South Africans visiting the Western Cape were heading for Cape Town with its prime attractions Victoria & Alfred Waterfront (entertainment and shopping centre), the beaches, Table Mountain or the Cape of Good Hope and only 3% staying over in the neighboring Winelands. But more than half of domestic tourists extended their explorations to more than their prime destination region with the Winelands due to its proximity taking almost half (45%) of this secondary provincial tourist distribution. Among the pull factors of the Winelands the highest importance was accredited to the wine industry (89%), while cultural history (45%) and mountain hiking in the mountain reserves (40%) are strong secondary attractions (WCTB, 1999). It is assumed that in 1998 the 1.2 million South Africans visiting the Western Cape spent about R 4.2 billions, topped up by 0.5 million intra-provincial tourists to about R 4.8 billions, while the 0.83 million overseas tourist spent 7.2 billions so that the provincial tourism turnover amounted to R 12 billions

(WCTB, 1999; Western Cape Province, 1999) of which Stellenbosch secured a share of just under 10%.

Throughout the second half of the 1990s surveys conducted by the national tourism board confirmed that for overseas tourists eight out of the ten most visited South African attractions were based in the Western Cape although it makes up only a tenth of the country. Of the 1.48 million overseas tourists in 1998 more than half (56%) visited this province with–similar to the patterns in domestic tourism–the three prime destinations all situated within the metropolitan area of Cape Town: The undisputed front runner throughout the 1990s being the Victoria & Alfred Waterfront visited by half (50%) of the international visitors followed by the peninsula of the Cape of Good Hope and then Table Mountain. As the most important international attraction outside the city the provincial wine routes ranked fourth which were visited by a third (35%) of all overseas tourists while the international trademark Kruger National Park trailed with 16% being only seventh on the list (SATOUR, 1998; Western Cape Province, 1999).

Although the Winelands and especially Stellenbosch boast a rich and well preserved cultural history the notorious "beaten track" of overseas visitors "touring the Winelands" usually looks like this: Coming on a day trip (from the Cape Town area) in an (organized or private) group and "doing" the wine route(s) chiefly in Stellenbosch (because it is closest to Cape Town) by calling at an estate or cellar and tasting possibly at a second one before "exploring" the city centre along Dorp Street with its national monuments and a rush through the Village Museum (2-3 hours) before heading either back home or continuing to a wine farm of the neighboring wine routes of Paarl or Franschhoek and leaving back a low occupancy rate of the only about 3,050 guest beds in the district. Of the domestic visitors more than half only stop at the estates or cellars and do not come into town at all–either because they have been here before or are not interested in cultural history.

DOMINATING LANDSCAPE AND TOURISM: THE STELLENBOSCH WINE INDUSTRY

Although Stellenbosch is one of the smallest among the fifteen South African wine districts, its about 600 square km afoot of mountain ranges rising up to 1,400 meters makes up for more than a sixth (16,112 ha or 15.3%) of the national hectarage of vineyards dominating the local land use pattern (SAWIS, 2001). From the varietal composition the Stellenbosch district is the only one in South Africa with a dominance of the red varieties (55%) with the most important ones being Cabernet Sauvignon (19.2%), Merlot (9.9%), Pinotage (9.5%) and Shiraz (9.2%). For white wines Chenin Blanc (17.6%) and Sauvignon Blanc (12.3%) are by far the dominant varieties (SAWIS, 2001: 6, 10). In 2000 just over 200 farms in the district had planted vineyards commercially, but only 106 marketed products under their own labels (STIB, 2001) while the rest sold the harvest to local co-operatives and/or producing wholesalers. Some of the latter are traditionally based in Stellenbosch adding to the importance of its vino-economic complex, such as Distell which owns or has substantial shares in about three dozen wine farms, estates or marketing brands mainly in the Stellenbosch area and is responsible for just under 30% of the Western Cape's good wine production (van Zyl, 2002).

While wine consumers around the globe think of Stellenbosch as *the* red-wine producing area in South Africa many of its white, sparkling and fortified wines feature prominently in the premier league too. According to the authoritative wine guide "John Platter South African Wines" for red wines of the 1996 to 2000 vintages 179 or 61% of the 294 highest national accolades were awarded to Stellenbosch (estate) wines as well as 82 or 46% of the 177 for white wines of the 1998 to 2000 vintages while fortified wines took "only" 3 of the 36 gold medals awarded (van Zyl, 2002). The key contributors to this excellence in quality are the generally mild Mediterranean climate with annual rainfalls of 600-800 mm, variegated soil types and the cooling breezes off the close by False Bay at the back of the Cape Peninsula which help to moderate the summer temperatures effectively (SAWID, 2000; van Zyl, 2002).

A tour of Burgundy in the 1960s made two owners of Stellenbosch wine estates, Frans Malan of Simonsig and Neil Joubert of Spier, think that the establishment of a French style wine route would be an ideal marketing tool to boost both quality and sales of the Cape wine industry. Drumming up support among local estate owners and overcoming the inevitable hesitations and practical problems as well as necessary amendments to the liquor laws, the Stellenbosch Wine Route officially opened in April 1971. It proved such a tremendous success with domestic and overseas visitors that it not only grew up to 42 members in 2000, with 21 conducting winery tours and 15 offering fully fledged restaurant services (STIB, 2001), but also triggered the creation of wine routes in all the fourteen other wine districts of South Africa. Nevertheless, due to the predominance of a Calvinist culture and the restricting regulations of the Liquor Act only three members of the Stellenbosch Wine Route were open for tasting and sales on Saturday afternoons and Sundays in 1999.

Although not the least for tax reasons, no figures are available regarding the share of the direct marketing in the wine sales of Stellenbosch producers. However, the author's investigations suggest that in recent years small estates depend for about a third to half of their turnover on over-the-counter sales with a substantial share of loyal domestic customers visiting regularly to top up their stocks or to overseas visitors enlarging their cabin hand luggage. With medium sized estates or cellars this dependence drops to about a tenth in average while for the big cellars and wholesalers the tasting, tours and direct marketing are *quantitées négligeable* as to the balance sheet but rather serve as important tools to strengthen the branding and customer relationship.

The 42 members of the Stellenbosch Wine Route nevertheless comprise only slightly more than a half of the 76 estates, wine farms, co-operatives and wholesalers locally more or less open to the general public in 1999 (see Table 1). In 1992 there were only 26 enterprises open for retail marketing. A survey conducted in that year suggested that an estimated number of about 516,000 visitors called at these enterprises. Only seven years later the number of wine farms, estates and cellars marketing directly to visitors tripled to 76 as has the number of visits to a total of about 1,672,000. Looking closer at the composition of this figure reveals that more than quarter of all visits were "swallowed" up by just one and only four year old enterprise, while half of the visitor numbers are distributed among only fifteen enterprises (Tourism Synergy, 2000). The pool of the local wine tourism industry obviously is populated with a few sharks and many small fishes. The market research conducted in 1992 established that the average journey to the vineyards of Stellenbosch stopped at 3.9 enterprises bringing the number of visitors to the region down to about 107,000. The 1999 figures indicate that the average of stops has dropped slightly to 3.5 resulting in about 478,000 true visitors, nevertheless indicating an increase of 447% in less than a decade (Tourism Synergy, 2000). However, it must be stated that most of the enterprises only estimated the number of visitors they received.

SPIER RESORT:
CASE STUDY OF AN INNOVATIVE HYBRID CONCEPT IN WINE TOURISM DEVELOPMENT

Recent global trends in leisure and tourism which favoring multifunctional and theme-park like packaged experiences also spill over into the Cape wine tourism. The pioneering role-model in a post-modern merger of traditional estate wine tourism and Disneyesque family holi-day resorts in South Africa is Spier Resort, a few kilometers to the south west of Stellenbosch. Although still a newcomer it immediately secured the "top dog" position among the wine tourism enterprises not only in Stellenbosch but in the whole Winelands Spier by drawing more than a quarter of the visits at all publicly accessible estates, wine farms, co-op-eratives and wholesalers in the wine district of Stellenbosch. If not for this exceptional size the innovative hybrid tourism concept behind this tremendous success is worth a case study highlighting the current (wine) tourism trends about to transform the traditional mono-thematic tourism in the Stellenbosch vineyards.

The farmlands of Spier were granted already in 1692 and when in 1712 it was transferred to another German settler he named the farm in honour of his birth place Speyer. In time this town on the river Rhine faded in memory and the name transformed to Spier which in Dutch has the meaning for reed, which seemed appropriate for the wet marshes along the small rivers on the farm.

In 1993, after three centuries of rather unspectacular farming includ-ing vineyards and wine making, the South African investor Dick Enthoven bought the estate from the Joubert family, once one of the co-founders of the Stellenbosch Wine Route, and started what has turned out to become by far the biggest tourism development ever launched in the Winelands. The attraction profile of Spier Resort, opened with its first phase in 1995 and owned by a holding of various sub-companies with a dominance of a few non-public share holding companies, was designed especially to target the main market of the Winelands, Capetonians on a wine or leisure expedition, to whom the complex with its slogan of *"unexpected pleasures"* now often serves as a one-stop for all their needs. By this Spier functions rather unintention-ally but effectively as a *cordon sanitaire*–or as the Stellenboschians unaffectionately put it, a vacuum-cleaner–to absorb a big chunk of the increasing day visitor numbers to the Stellenbosch vineyards and thereby contributing more than acknowledged by the locals to preserve the tra-ditional small scale structure of the wine tourism from undesired trans-formation by general overcrowding.

The Spier Resort, mainly consisting of the farms of Spier and De Zalze between the hamlets of Lynedoch and Jamestown at the south western edge of Stellenbosch, comprises about 1,000 ha and is the larg-est private landholding in the Stellenbosch Municipality. These grounds are managed–and marketed for the eco-minded segment of tourism–as an eco-friendly home to an integrated and sustainable agricultural and

TABLE 1. Estimated Visitorship to Wine Farms, Estates, Co-Operatives and Wholesalers in the Stellenbosch Area Listing Enterprises with at Least 2,000 Visitors in the Year 1999

Name of enterprise	absolute figure of visitors	percent share in total visitors	cummulative figures of visitors	
			absolute	percent share
Spier Resort & Cellar*	450,000	26.92		
Delheim*	130,000	7.78		
Stellenbosch Farmers Winery (SFW)*	105,000	6.28		
Simonsig*	80,000	4.78		
Vergelegen	74,000	4.43	839,000	50.18
Hartenberg*	62,000	3.71		
Muratie*	50,000	2.99		
Delaire*	47,000	2.81		
Eikendal*	43,320	2.59		
Blaauwklippen*	40,000	2.39		
Welmoed*	40,000	2.39		
Neethlingshof*	37,000	2.21		
Morgenhof*	36,000	2.15		
Vlottenburg Wine Cellar*	35,000	2.09		
Zevenwacht*	35,000	2.09	1,264,320	75.62
Helderberg*	30,000	1.79		
Warwick	30,000	1.79		
Louiesenhof*	25,000	1.50		
Bergkelder Wine Cellar	23,561	1.41		
Kanonkop	23,400	1.40		
Overgaauw*	22,000	1.32		
Rust-en-Vrede*	18,720	1.12		
Eersterivier*	16,800	1.00		
J.C. le Roux House of Champagne	15,447	0.92		
L'Avenir*	15,000	0.90		
Saxenburg*	13,560	0.81		
Thelema	12,000	0.72		
Hazendal*	10,000	0.60		
Jordan*	10,000	0.60		
Lanzerac*	9,500	0.57		
Bottelary*	9,385	0.56		
Fort Simon*	8,700	0.52		
Koelenhof Winery	8,600	0.51		
Louisvale*	8,000	0.48		
Kaapzicht	7,200	0.43		
Verdun (since renamed Asara)*	7,150	0.43		
Uitkyk	7,000	0.42		
Vredenheim*	6,500	0.39		

Alto	5,000	0.30		
Le Bonheur	5,000	0.30		
Longridge	5,000	0.30		
Middelvlei*	5,000	0.30		
Rustenberg	5,000	0.30		
Uiterwyk*	4,400	0.26		
Lievland*	4,300	0.26		
Mulderbosch	4,100	0.25		
Vriesenhof & Talana Hill	4,000	0.24		
Audacia	3,650	0.22		
Avontuur	3,650	0.22		
Rozendal	3,500	0.21		
Bredell	2,600	0.16		
Beyerskloof & Bouwland	2,400	0.14		
Laibach	2,000	0.12	1,661,660	99.38

plus 21 wine farms and estates (including 9 wine route members) with less than 2.000 visitors each and a total of 10.340 or 0,62 % of all visitors

(* = Member of Stellenbosch Wine Route)

Sources: Stellenbosch Tourism & Information Bureau (2000): Stellenbosch and its Wine Route: 3; Tourism Synergy 2000: 58-61; amendments and rectifications by author

tourism resort enterprise. Portions of the farmland are set aside as maintained or rehabilitated natural areas for ecological corridors along river beds to be integrated in the proposed Boland Biosphere Reserve to protect the unique but endangered Cape Floral Kingdom (only 0.006% of the global land surface but about 5,500 species with a substantial share of endemic plants). According to its vision "to create a sustainable ecology" all developments at Spier strive to adhere as closely as possible to environmentally friendly but yet economically sustainable principles (Dennis Moss, 2001).

In 2001 the still unfolding Spier Resort complex comprised of about one and a half dozen interlocked attractions physically developed in a blend of the traditional Cape Dutch and Victorian styles. Using the historic farmstead and the oldest dated wine cellar (1780) in the province only as the corner stone for a new hybrid agro-tourism concept the facilities try to create the desired unique "Spier experience" by adding investment intensive attractions of a different sort to the traditional wine-gastronomy product. By providing unprecedented leisure attractions Spier immediately catapulted itself to be the undisputed leader in a wine tourism scene lacking new marketing ideas since the inception of the wine route concept. Currently, the leisure complex at Spier Resort includes:

- a wine tasting centre in the old cape dutch barn to sell the resort's own award wining estate wines (currently about 80 ha vineyards are planted) and as one-stop wine shop featuring more than 200 local and 30 overseas wine estates,
- a diversified gastronomy including three major restaurants, a coffee shop and a tea garden with picnic area in a landscaped area with a "picnic basket" service.
- entertainment venues including the restored and refurbished old "Manor House" for a historic experience, a conference and banqueting centre as well as an open-air 1,400 seats amphitheater for all sorts of cultural events including the "Spier Festival" in summer (November-March) with prime cultural events,
- a railway station along the line between Cape Town and Stellenbosch with its own vintage train to serve as exclusive shuttle for major cultural events or conferences,
- a nature experience complex consisting of the "Cape Raptor World" to reintroduce extinct or severely endangered regional birds of prey and a cheetah park with breeding programme,
- an emerging sport complex including an equestrian centre with stables for 30 horses and six tennis courts with a (planned) tennis academy,
- a 155-room four-star hotel in 32 double story buildings currently being by far the biggest accommodation enterprise in the Winelands.

In the strive for "sustainability through economic viability, social development and environmental integrity" Spier houses activities which indirectly contribute to the tourism product such as the Institute for Culinary Arts, an educational centre for chefs and 40 ha of organic vegetable farming supplying, along with contract farmers, an on-site distribution centre to market daily up to 3 tons of fresh produce into the regional markets as well as support programmes for emerging local organic farmers. In order to ensure environmental and social sustainable impact of these major tourism developments Spier has pledged itself to the principles of substantial benefits to the local communities and the maintenance or rehabilitation of cultural and natural resources (Dennis Moss, 2001: 52-53; Mr. Gareth Haysom on 14.3.2002). Under consideration or in the process of planning are routes for mountain bikers, cultural tourism activities around a proposed Khoi (museum) village with African arts and crafts and a botanical garden. Far flung ideas even envisage a Spier Film Studio.

As to leisure and tourism this wide range of activities explicitly tries to accommodate three related but different markets:

1. Day visitors from the Cape Town metropolitan area (2.5 million inhabitants) and the neighboring towns of the Winelands, Breede River and Overberg regions (0.4 million inhabitants) with a still rather exceptional customer orientated opening policy of seven days a week all year around;
2. Domestic and international overnight visitors on a leisure trip with overseas demand relatively constant except for the off-season in Winter while domestic visitors peak during the South African school holidays especially in December/January and Easter;
3. Conferences and functions by a wide range of business and leisure amenities and the proximity of Cape Town within a reach of 30 minutes.

As regards to marketing Spier as yet has not made significant impact outside the Cape and the domestic core markets–not the least due to the fact that the Western Cape Province still lacks overseas tourism marketing facilities which proved so instrumental with international competitors like the tourism representatives of the Australian states working the European core markets. Nevertheless, Spier identified "branding" as one the immediate necessities, and to work at least the domestic markets more intensively has established as a show case a wine shop at Sun City, the South African version of Las Vegas north west of the national economic power house Gauteng.

The next and so far biggest development at Spier currently realized on the eastern half of the farmland is a 18-hole golf course, the third one in Stellenbosch, in combination with a country club and financed through the subdivision and building of 463 resort units in a landscaped village environment to be sold to investors and another 250-room 4- or 5-star-hotel to be managed by Ritz-Carlton (Dennis Moss, 2001). In the short term therefore the leisure management of Spier targets the domestic up market tourism sector focusing on conferencing, golf and incentive tourism and utilising its location in the popular Winelands, the character of a "wine estate," numerous on-site amenities and the proximity to Cape Town and its airport as key selling points. On the overseas markets Spier's hopes rest with its so far unrivalled accommodation resources amidst the small scaled hotel industry of the Winelands to attract more self drive tourism, currently brought in by contracts with European travel companies like DER-Tours of Germany, and tour groups looking for an alternative overnight location outside but close to the urbanised Cape Metropolitan Area (Dennis Moss, 2001; Mr. Gareth Haysom on 14.3.2002).

The measurable impact of the only seven year old Spier Resort on the wine route tourism in Stellenbosch is therefore enormous; it makes up for more than a quarter of all wine route stops and offers about a tenth of all beds (soon to be increased to a sixth) in the area generating a leisure turnover of about R 50 millions or about 5% of the tourism generated total turnover of Stellenbosch. Already now with about 1,000 jobs–600 permanent and 400 seasonal workers–of which about 600 can be attributed to the activities of the tourism and leisure sectors (Mr. Gareth Haysom on 14.3.2002), it is the by far biggest tourism employer not only in Stellenbosch but the Winelands district.

CONCLUSION

The interdependent rise of wine and tourism at the Cape was an immediate result of the departure of apartheid. This sparked off a sustained boom in the wine industry which has developed into an agricultural mono-structure in terms of land use, employment and turn over. While being an industry in its own right, viticulture at the Cape twinned with tourism today represents the prime non-urban tourist attraction for foreign visitors to South Africa. To market its produce increasingly both in quantity and quality the wine industry has proactively taken advantage of this opportunity and opened up new channels to supplement the traditional domestic retail network.

Recent marketing trends in the Stellenbosch wine district clearly show the key importance of a revised customer relationship to secure sufficient shares in the growing leisure and tourist market. Powerful tools are a formerly unknown "open cellar"-policy, branding efforts to spur export promotion among returning overseas tourists and introducing "additional values" to a visit to wine enterprises. The post-modern spearhead in the Winelands and possible role-model for follow-ups in this direction is Spier Resort. This massive hybrid investment "disguised" as an old fashioned wine estate offers an innovative multifunctional blend of more or less wine-related attractions and activities to catch as much as possible of the *en vogue* market niches in high class leisure and tourism.

In general terms the most threatening recent developments which may spoil the bright picture for wine and tourism in the Winelands and especially Stellenbosch are the massive and still rising labor migration from South Africa's overpopulated rural provinces creating urban sprawl in the neighboring metropolitan area and unemployment with its pertaining crime problem that already threatens the regional tourism industry In the longer term certainly the friction deriving from the fact that both the wine and tourism industries are still "white man" dominated with few black and colored entrepreneurs (and tourists) having emerged in the first decade of the self declared "rainbow nation."

AUTHOR NOTE

Information supplied by *Mr. Gareth Haysom*, Executive Director: Leisure of *Spier Resort Management (Pty.) Limited*, in an interview on 14.3.2002.

ENDNOTE

1. Throughout the 1990s the South African currency Rand (R) experienced an accelerating devaluation against the US dollar with the following average rates per one US dollar: 1994-R 3.5; 1996-R 4.3; 1998-R 5.5; 2000-R 7.8; March 2002-R 12.2.

REFERENCES

Bulpin, T.V. (1994). *Illustrated Guide to Southern Africa*. Fifth edition. Cape Town.
Cape of Good Hope Bank/Western Cape Investment and Trade Promotion Agency [*WESGRO*] (1999). *Western Cape Economic Monitor*, 11/1999, 6.
Demhardt, I.J. (2000): Aktuelle Strukturen in der tourismusgeographischen Entwicklung des Binnen- und Auslandstourismus der Western Cape Province (Südafrika). In J. Bähr & U. Jürgens (eds.) *Transformationprozesse im Südlichen Afrika*. Kiel: Kieler Geographische Schriften 104, 173-190.
Demhardt, I.J. (2003). Vom apartheidstaat zur regenbogennation. Bedeutung, struktur, nachfrage und probleme des tourismus in Südafrika. In C. Becker, A. Steinecke & H. Hopfinger (eds.), *Handbuch der Geographie der Freizeit und des Tourismus*. München (in print).
Dennis Moss Partnership (2001). *Spier De Zalze Precinct Development Framework*. Stellenbosch, unpublished consultative draft, Dennis Moss Partnership.
Leibold, M. & Steyn, J.N. (1998). *Loodsstudie vir bepaling van die ekonomiese impak van toerisme op Stellenbosch en omgewing*, unpublished report, Bellvill.

South African Tourism Board [*SATOUR*] (1998). *A Survey of South Africa's International Tourism Market. Summer 1998*. Pretoria: South African Tourism Board.

SA Wine Industry Directory [*SAWID*] (2000). *SA Wine Industry Directory 2000*, Cape Town: Ampersand Press & Wynboer Magazine & VinPro SA.

South African Wine Industry Information & Systems [*SAWIS*] (2001). *South African Wine Industry Statistics, No. 25*. Paarl: South African Wine Industry Information & Systems.

Stellenbosch Tourism & Information Bureau [*STIB*] (2001). *Official Tourism Guide to Stellenbosch & its Wine Route. Tourist Guide 2001*. Stellenbosch: Stellenbosch Tourism & Information Bureau.

Tourism Synergy Limited (March 2000). *Tourism Management Plan for the Stellenbosch Area. Phase 1: Situation Analysis*, unpublished consultative report. Stellenbosch: Tourism Synergy Limited.

van Zyl, P. (ed.) (2002). *John Platters South African Wines 2002. A Guide to Cellars, Vineyards, Winemakers, Restaurants and Accommodation*. Cape Town.

Western Cape Investment and Trade Promotion Agency [*WESGRO*] (2001). *Cape Sector Factsheet–The Wine Industry in the Western Cape*. Cape Town: Western Cape Investment and Trade Promotion Agency.

Western Cape Province, Department of Economic Affairs, Agriculture and Tourism (1999). *Western Cape Tourism Green Paper*. Cape Town: Western Cape Province, Department of Economic Affairs, Agriculture and Tourism.

Western Cape Tourism Board [*WCTB*] (1999). *Market Survey–Travel Patterns of Domestic Tourists*, unpublished report. Cape Town: Western Cape Tourism Board.

Wiese, B. (1999). *Südafrika mit Lesotho und Swaziland*. Stuttgart: Gotha.

Policy, Support and Promotion for Food-Related Tourism Initiatives: A Marketing Approach to Regional Development

Steven Boyne
Derek Hall
Fiona Williams

SUMMARY. Increasingly, regional tourism development initiatives are utilizing locally-produced foodstuffs and beverages to: strengthen areas' tourism products; enhance visitors' experiences; and help maintain and enhance the viability of local food production and processing sectors. This paper examines the ways in which food and tourism are being drawn together at a theoretical level by academics, at a strategic level by policy makers, and at an applied level by developers and practitioners. While the marketing philosophy provides a useful framework for the planning and management of food-related tourism initiatives, adopting

Steven Boyne is Researcher, Leisure and Tourism Management Department, Derek Hall is Head, Leisure and Tourism Management Department, and Professor of Regional Development, Fiona Williams is Researcher, Rural Policy Group, all at the Scottish Agricultural College (SAC).

Address correspondence to: Steven Boyne, Leisure and Tourism Management Department, SAC Ayr Campus, Auchincruive, KA6 5HW, Scotland, United Kingdom (E-mail: S.Boyne@au.sac.ac.uk).

[Haworth co-indexing entry note]: "Policy, Support and Promotion for Food-Related Tourism Initiatives: A Marketing Approach to Regional Development." Boyne, Steven, Derek Hall, and Fiona Williams. Co-published simultaneously in *Journal of Travel & Tourism Marketing* (The Haworth Hospitality Press, an imprint of The Haworth Press, Inc.) Vol. 14, No. 3/4, 2003, pp. 131-154; and: *Wine, Food, and Tourism Marketing* (ed: C. Michael Hall) The Haworth Hospitality Press, an imprint of The Haworth Press, Inc., 2003, pp. 131-154. Single or multiple copies of this article are available for a fee from The Haworth Document Delivery Service [1-800-HAWORTH, 9:00 a.m. - 5:00 p.m. (EST). E-mail address: docdelivery@haworthpress.com].

10.1300/J073v14n03_08   *131*

such an approach is problematic owing to a shortfall in our understanding of consumer behavior with regard to food in the context of leisure and tourism. In the absence of such knowledge, and in the light of the positive economic and social benefits which such initiatives can create, this paper examines the ways in which food-related tourism initiatives are being promoted using the World Wide Web. The research highlights inadequacies in the web-based promotion of food-related tourism initiatives in the UK and suggests that, while this type of tourism is at an early stage in the product life-cycle (in the UK), these shortcomings are also due in part to the fragmented infrastructure for regional tourism development and promotion in the UK. Additionally, practical recommendations are made as regards design factors for the provision of web-based tourism information. *[Article copies available for a fee from The Haworth Document Delivery Service: 1-800-HAWORTH. E-mail address: <docdelivery@haworthpress. com> Website: <http://www.HaworthPress.com> © 2003 by The Haworth Press, Inc. All rights reserved.]*

KEYWORDS. Tourism, food production, gastronomy, Internet, marketing, promotion, regional development

BACKGROUND, RATIONALE AND AIMS

Increasingly–and not least in rural regions with transitional economies–gastronomy-related heritage is being employed to strengthen areas' tourism products. In many cases development initiatives explicitly seek to deliver benefits for both the tourism and food-related industry sectors by creating and strengthening "back-linkages", between these (e.g., Telfer & Wall, 1996; Boyne et al., 2002). In this way, high-quality food and beverage products can enhance the overall tourism product and tourists' experiences, while tourism-related spending on these locally-produced goods provides economic stimuli to maintain or reinvigorate the viability of the local primary production and processing sectors.

The interrelationships between tourism and food are being recognised and explored by academic researchers and built upon by policy makers and planners engaged in regional economic development. The drawing together of policy for tourism and food production in rural areas can be seen to represent the shifting emphasis in the way in which governance for rural development is being reconceived–from a sectorally-based approach, to a territorially-based one.

However, more research-orientated work is required to guide those engaged in implementing the type of food-related tourism initiative described above. Elsewhere, we have identified a research gap–or more accurately, a meeting ground between approaches to food-related tourism research– where more data would be welcome (Boyne et al., 2002). In this paper, we note that a marketing philosophy (marketing-orientation) approach allows us to articulate this knowledge gap in terms of the requirement for an integrated approach to product development and promotion.

Unfortunately, adopting a marketing philosophy approach to the implementation of food-related tourism developments is problematic owing to: (i) a lack of adequate understanding of consumer behavior as regards food in the context of leisure and tourism (Fields, 2002); and (ii) ambiguities surrounding the way in which food production is conceived by consumers and the realities of modern food production regimes. It is possible, however, to examine the ways in which food- and gastronomy-related tourism initiatives are being promoted. Following an inductive research approach, we have noted inadequacies in the web-based promotion of food-related tourism initiatives–the resulting research undertaken for this paper has identified that these inadequacies are borne to some extent out of the cleavage between product development and promotion in terms of the structure of institutional support for rural tourism development in the United Kingdom (UK).

This paper, therefore, describes the development context for food-related tourism initiatives in the UK, and against this background–which points to a convergence of food production and rural tourism in theoretical and policy related terms–it identifies that such a convergence remains to be realized at a practical implementation level. The authors argue that, while such inadequacies will stem in part from the early evolutionary point in the product life cycle at which food-related tourism initiatives in the UK are currently positioned, there is a requirement for a clearer definition of roles for support organisations and a framework for these organisations to work efficaciously together to achieve the effective implementation of strategies.

In addition, the authors propose a four-fold theoretical taxonomy of consumers based on the importance of food and gastronomy in their destination decision-making processes. Using this taxonomy as an analytical framework, recommendations are made regarding best practice in providing web-based destination information for consumers. These recommendations are germane in the wider tourism context and can be applied to other forms of holiday activity promotion.

TOURISM, FOOD AND GASTRONOMY

Currently, there is a growing recognition of the relationships between tourism, food and gastronomy. The publication of one of the first texts dedicated to this subject area (Richards & Hjalager, 2002) endorses the strength of this relationship and, within that (edited) text, the range and diversity of affinities between these areas is highlighted. One fundamental similarity, for example, is the way in which both the food and tourism industries are experiencing growth in mass-scale production–often to the detriment of artisanal and small-scale production–and, somewhat in opposition to this, how these sectors have found in each other potential solutions to these problems (Hjalager & Richards, 2002).

As described above, solutions are often based around development initiatives where these sectors link at a local or regional level to provide reciprocal benefits: local foodstuffs enhance and strengthen the tourism product while tourists and visitors provide a market for these products. Additional benefits can include the formation of external markets for local produce, generated by tourists upon their return home and facilitated by creating locally-based strategic alliances amongst the food production and processing sectors.

While the individual contributions to Richards and Hjalager's (2002) text have been undertaken largely from a tourism studies perspective, one contributor, Scarpato (2002), calls for a gastronomy studies approach to gastronomic tourism and to tourism in general. Gastronomy studies is described as an emerging and multi-disciplinary perspective which seeks to enhance the gastronomic life of communities with a view to environmental and social sustainability. Such an approach should, Scarpato suggests, be commensurate with the critical theory approach, in this way representing the previously subverted voice of gastronomy-related studies in academia and valorizing gastronomic issues within the context of tourism and tourism development. Scarpato (2002) cites Symons (1999, p. 333) who writes that gastronomy, most simply, is "the study of meals" and that gastronomy and tourism studies intersect to some degree as they are both "concerned with meals." Elsewhere in the same text, however, from their analysis of tourism research literature dealing with food-related issues, the authors of this paper (Boyne et al., 2002) have identified several other ways in which tourism and gastronomy studies can be seen to intersect.

Tourism and Food Interrelationships

Boyne et al.'s (2002) taxonomy of tourism and food interrelationships, illustrated in Figure 1, describes four interrelated domains; these represent a conceptual disaggregation of the approaches that have been taken in academic, tourism studies-orientated, analyses of tourism and food interrelationships.

Using this taxonomy as an organizing framework, we have argued that future research should prioritise areas with the greatest immediate relevance to planners, policy makers and practitioners. Specifically, we recommend an initial focus on Domains I and IV. Within Domain I, the *direct production-related* (DPR) domain, papers typically deal with issues such as:

* agri-and horticultural food production and management systems;
* food processing;
* supply chain management; and
* impacts of tourism on destination areas' food production.

While Domain IV, the *indirect consumption-related* (ICR) domain, describes work that deals with, for example:

* tourists' consumption of agricultural landscapes and settings;
* food as a destination image component or marketing/promotion tool; and
* consumption of agri-tourism products and services such as farm parks and visitor attractions.

Elsewhere, research papers in Domain III (*direct consumption-related*) deal mainly with catering and hospitality-related issues while in

FIGURE 1. Tourism and Food Interrelationships

Production-related	Consumption-related
I Direct production-related (DPR)	III Direct consumption-related (DCR)
II Indirect production-related (IPR)	IV Indirect consumption-related (ICR)

Source: after Boyne et al. (2002)

Domain II (*indirect production-related*), studies have investigated structural factors such as landscape maintenance and creation. There has also been *post-hoc* research focussing on the interactions between the tourism and food production sectors in relation to their use of and demand for land, labor and capital (see Boyne et al., 2002, for further details).

So, from this examination of the tourism research literature, several dimensions in which tourism and food issues intersect have been identified and recommendations for future research foci have been drawn from this. The two areas identified for future research are concerned largely with product development (Domain I) and promotional activities (Domain IV). These areas are, of course, two aspects of the marketing philosophy approach.

It can be seen, then, that: the relationships between tourism and food have been approached from a variety of perspectives within the field of tourism studies; the eclectic and trans-disciplinary gastronomy studies could, equally, operate within each of the four domains in the taxonomy above; and the marketing philosophy approach also provides an appropriate overarching framework for addressing food-related tourism development initiatives in so far as it provides an ideal framework within which to draw together product development and promotion-related issues, that is, Domains I and IV as described above.

Policy for Development

It is not only within the academy, however, that these relationships have been recognized. Recently, in the UK, strategy documents for rural development, agriculture and tourism have endorsed the strength of the relationship between the tourism and food production sectors. The rural white paper for England, *Our Countryside: The future. A fair deal for rural England* (DETR, 2000, p. 84) notes that: "Tourism can also help other rural industries. Businesses who provide eating and catering services for tourists are well placed to promote regional food and drink products, benefiting local producers, as well as improving the interest of an area to visitors."

While, in Scotland, the *Forward Strategy for Scottish Agriculture* (Scottish Executive, 2001, p. 23) recommends that rural land-based businesses may seek new opportunities through greater integration with the tourism industry, and goes on to say: "There is a real need to improve the quality of tourism in Scotland; it is vital that we develop better links between these two important sectors so that farmers can earn income from this tourism and, in turn, can help to ensure that we provide the quality infrastructure and services required by visitors to Scotland" (p. 23).

Tourism policy documents include: *Tomorrow's Tourism* (DCMS, 1999), which encourages British tourism businesses to source and promote locally-produced foodstuffs (p. 67, 100); *Working for the Countryside* (English Tourism Council, 2001), which emphasises the need to "promote local produce and gastronomy" (p. 3); and, in Scotland, the *Tourism Framework for Action: 2002-2005* document makes clear that, to maximise tourism's benefits, it is necessary to build: ". . . stronger links between tourism and sectors such as retail, food and drink and transport that have a major influence on the tourism 'experience', and which also benefit from tourism" (Scottish Executive, 2002, p. 19).

This policy-level fusion of rural tourism and food production/agriculture has been underpinned not only by the recognition of the strength of synergy between these sectors of economic activity, but also by a groundshift in approaches to rural development and regional governance in the UK. This shift is typified by the re-emerging perspective in policy for regional planning and development, which views rural development as a territorial rather than a sectoral issue. In Scotland, since Parliamentary devolution in 1999, the former Scottish Office Agriculture, Environment and Fisheries Department (SOAEFD) has become the Scottish Executive Environment and Rural Affairs Department (SEERAD) headed by a Minister for Rural Affairs. In Wales, devolution has led to the creation of the Agriculture Department and a Department for Urban and Rural Development, with the former overseen by a "Secretary for Agriculture and Rural Development," and in Northern Ireland, the Department for Agriculture and Rural Development is headed by a Minister with the same title. Following the Foot and Mouth Disease crisis of 2001, England has also witnessed the restructuring of its agricultural policy ministry from the Ministry for Agriculture, Fisheries and Food (MAFF) to the Department for Environment, Food and Rural Affairs (DEFRA).

Food Sector Development Initiatives

Just as government departments in the UK have recognized the linkages between tourism and food, so too have the agencies responsible for the promotion of regional food-related economic sectors. In England and Wales, the government-supported Food From Britain (FFB) organization includes as part of its mission a remit to foster the development of Britain's specialty food and drink sector (FFB, 2002a). To do this, it works alongside regional and county-based food groups in England and similar representative bodies in Wales, Scotland and Northern Ireland (there are ten of these groups in England and four covering the remainder of the UK, that is: Scotland; Northern Ireland; Wales; and the Isle of Wight–see FFB, 2002b, for details). It is not unusual for these *local food and drink groups* to have created tourism-related promotional material, in some cases in collaboration with Regional Development Agencies (RDAs) in England and Wales, Local Enterprise Companies (LECs) in Scotland, Local Authorities (LAs) and non-government agencies (NGOs). What is less frequently seen, however, are examples where these food and tourism initiatives constitute (either wholly or in part) a strategic approach to regional development in which the tourism and food sectors are brought together specifically to enhance the tourism product and stimulate tourism-induced economic activity in the local production and processing sectors.

Such bi-directional approaches to regional development have demonstrated some success. Telfer (2000), for example, has described ways in which the *Tastes of Niagara* programme in Southern Ontario, Canada has generated positive outcomes for that area. This "Quality Food Alliance" between the Niagara Region's food producers, processors, distributors, hotels, restaurants, wineries and chefs has been successful in raising the profile of the regional cuisine of Niagara. The organization developed from a project by the Agri-Hospitality Committee of a non-profit, volunteer organization, *Vision Niagara Planning and Development Inc.*, and dates from 1993. The partnership approach to working has improved communications between members of the Alliance and consumers (via publicity materials) and has contributed to reducing economic leakages by creating a greater reliance on local food among food and beverage users. Smaller farm and non-farm businesses which are a part of the Alliance have benefited from the opportunity to overcome barriers to direct marketing and this has helped them to remain competitive. Finally, the potential for new markets for local producers has been created by exposing consumers to regional foods and wines.

In Scotland, Boyne et al. (2001, 2002) have examined the *Isle of Arran Taste Trail* and found benefits similar to those described above. During 2000, Argyll and the Islands Enterprise (AIE)–the Local Enterprise Company responsible for implementing the *Trail*–undertook a survey of visitors to the area who had purchased the *Trail* guidebook. This survey revealed that, having read the guidebook, visitors to Arran were: (a) prepared to spend more money on meals consisting of locally produced food; (b) had been encouraged them to eat out more often; (c) would be more inclined in the future to purchase locally-produced groceries; and (d) indicated that the quality of Arran's food would be a positive factor in their decision to make a return visit to the island.

A complementary survey of *Trail* members found that the initiative had, for some businesses: (a) helped generate increased turnover and profit; (b) contributed to increases in volume of food prepared and sold; (c) contributed to increased catering-related customer spend per head; and (d) in one case had led to a lengthening of the tourism season by generating additional interest about the island. Significantly, the initiative can be seen to contribute to sustainable development objectives (Boyne et al., 2001). In particular, it: is small-scale; spreads the benefits widely throughout the area's economic sectors; may contain an intergenerational element (through family succession of businesses)–in this way promoting social sustainability; fosters community participation through the generation of strategic alliances; and is ultimately based on a renewable resource base–locally produced foodstuffs.

MARKETING AND PROMOTION

In view of the variety of positive impacts, described above, which it is possible for food-related tourism initiatives to generate, the necessity to enhance the viability of these through effective promotion is underlined. Indeed, in the UK, the rural white paper for England, *Our Countryside: The future. A fair deal for rural England* (DETR, 2000, p. 84) has stressed the importance of promotional and marketing efforts in successfully achieving growth in rural tourism-related sectors.

Marketing-Related Issues

Applying a marketing philosophy approach to the promotional dimension of food-related initiatives is, however, problematic. A limited amount of work has been undertaken investigating the ways in which consumers perceive regional foods in the UK: for example, Kuznesof et al. (1997) and Tregear et al. (1998) in a general context; and, specifically relating to tourists' attitudes, MAFF/CA (2000). Nevertheless, there exist large knowledge gaps relating to the way in which we understand consumer behaviour specifically as regards food in the context of leisure and tourism (Fields, 2002). For example, although images of food adorn many tourism-related promotional artefacts, the way in which visitors and potential visitors respond to these images is largely unknown. Additionally, while several sources in the tourism research literature tell us that food is an important aspect of the holiday experience (e.g., Marris, 1986; Choisy, 1996; Bessière, 1998, 2001)–or that it is not (Hudman, 1986)–it is difficult to find empirical information relating to *why* such results are to be found or about the role of food in consumers' destination decision-making processes.

This is because much of the research upon which these papers are based is either theoretically grounded, the findings are derived from *post hoc* assessments of consumers' holiday food experiences, or the outcomes are less widely applicable because of a specific focus on special interest tourists (for example, van Westering, 1999, or, in the context of wine tourism, Mitchell et al., 2000). Additionally, there is a lack of literature which describes how consumers view or experience specific kinds of food/beverage. In the tourism studies literature identified by these authors, for example, food and drink are considered to be a homogenous entity. While, elsewhere, in a non tourism-specific context, Kuznesof et al. (1997, p. 200), citing Skaggs et al. (1996), note that studies often investigate food products at an aggregate level alongside other product categories. Quantitative, tourism-related, work in this area is urgently required if food tourism product development and promotional efforts are to provide effectively what consumers seek.

The ways in which regionally-specific images are used in the promotion of specialty food has been analyzed recently by Kneafsey and Ilbery (2001). However, their investigation dealt with the producers' perspective. Their findings substantiate those of others working in this area, in so far as concepts of quality and regional images are socially constructed and contestable. For example, although promotional efforts attempt to convey notions of wholesomeness and tradition, it is acknowledged that in many cases there is no direct link between such narratives and actual food quality. Elsewhere, Hughes (1995a, 1995b) has noted this phenomenon, and describes "the erosion of the nature product link" (1995b, p. 117). Here Hughes describes the way in which marketers may utilize the notion that an area or region possesses some form of heritage in relation to the production of "quality" goods using "traditional" methods (with the underlying rationale that traditional = good). Such an approach may, however, conceal the fact that the "nature product link"–which once underpinned the quality of the produce–has been eroded or has even disappeared under the prevalent conditions afforded by modern, intensive farming regimes. One example of this is the labelling of Scottish smoked salmon which may describe the product as ". . . from the clear fresh waters of Scotland" or words to that effect–which, while not inaccurate, fails to convey to the consumer that the fish was reared intensively on a Scottish salmon farm.

Clark et al. (1994) suggest that, in a wider rural destination area promotional context, employing such imagery may be counterproductive and ultimately unsustainable as the proffered version of the "authentic countryside" often does not exist. What is more, if efforts to promote visits to rural areas are successful, then these areas' idyllic nature may be lost owing to the growing number of tourist arrivals. Consumers, however, may possess the ability to deal with this ambivalent relationship between promotional hyperbole and the nature of rural reality. Sørensen and Nilsson (2000) have found that while tourists in rural areas of Denmark demonstrate a high degree of awareness relating to issues such as farming methods, rural land-ownership and animal rights, the rural realities which such knowledge confers have not reduced their demand for tourism in the rural idyll.

The Research Approach

Nevertheless, while barriers and difficulties exist as regards implementing a marketing philosophy approach to the promotion of food-related tourism initiatives, it remains possible to assess and make recommendations regarding current promotional activities. This paper now goes on to critically evaluate the ways in which such development initiatives are being promoted using the World Wide Web as a medium–in particular, the authors focus on the ways in which information relating to local food initiatives is signposted by tourism information providers.

The authors have noted that while initiatives to promote local and regional food are often being developed with an emphasis on the tourism market, and in some cases have developed high-quality web sites, these web sites are (at the time of writing) less readily accessible to information-seeking consumers than they might otherwise be. Specifically, we are concerned that initiatives are often not suitably represented on the web sites of their respective official local tourist boards–i.e., the web sites that provide the point of departure for many consumers researching travel and holiday destinations. These web sites can either lack the appropriate hyperlinks, or have these "buried" deep within their site where they may not be discovered.

CURRENT PROVISION OF PROMOTIONAL MATERIAL

The World Wide Web as a Promotional Tool

The Internet has developed rapidly during recent years and can be used as an effective advertising and promotional tool, not least in the tourism and hospitality industry (Wan, 2002, p. 155). The Internet is, most basically, a large and global group of computers which are connected to one and other (Kristula, 2002a) with which ". . . users can send and receive e-mail, remotely login to other computers, participate in news groups and navigate the World Wide Web to browse and retrieve useful information" (Law, 2000, p. 66). As indicated by Law, the World Wide Web (WWW or Web) is not synonymous with the Internet: the Web can be described as that part of the Internet which can be accessed using web browser software such as Netscape Navigator and Microsoft Internet Explorer (two of the most popular web browsers) (Kristula, 2002b). The Web is made up of individual web pages and web sites (which host a collection of related pages) and navigation through and around these pages is facilitated by *hyperlinks*. These can be colored and/or underlined pieces of text, or graphic images, that the user can click on using their computer's mouse in order to have their browser software directed to the intended web page, web site or some other information which is accessible using another type of software (examples might include a word processed document or a spreadsheet document). Hyperlinks which move the browser around one particular web site are known as *internal* hyperlinks while those linking to other web sites are known as *external* hyperlinks. Web pages and sites often make use of a variety of multimedia applications which help them to be user friendly, entertaining or capable of providing information with a high level of sophistication.

Another application of the Internet–and one which is most usually undertaken using web-based facilities–is purchasing goods and services online. Although online sales continue to grow in various sectors of economic activity (for example, food and drink, financial services and leisure-related industries such as travel and hospitality and gambling), as regards tourism, the Web is most popularly used, at this time, as a research tool by consumers, whose researching may lead to a sale, but not necessarily an online one (Smith, 2002). For consumers, the Web can be extremely useful in this respect: it is possible to access a large variety of information about destinations often from more than one provider–an attribute which many consumers may welcome as they feel more able to choose their travel destination based on information from more than one source.

Tourism Information Provision on the Web

Many countries and regions now have dedicated tourism information web sites operated by or on behalf of national and/or regional tourism authorities. These sites provide the point of departure for many consumers seeking advice and information relating to prospective destinations. From our own experience of navigating the Web to source information relating to food-related tourism initiatives, however, we have noted that in many cases, although such an initiative exists and has a dedicated web site, it can be difficult, or at worst impossible, to find relevant information about, or hyperlinks to, these web sites from the respective national or regional tourist agency web sites.

The paper now goes on to briefly describe two examples of this in the UK (Figure 2)–and one example of good practice from Italy. Having described these examples, the authors introduce a theoretical taxonomy of consumers based on the importance of food and gastronomy in their destination decision-making processes. Using this taxonomy as an analytical framework, recommendations are made regarding ways in which links to food-related initiatives can be provided in such a way as to enhance the ease with which consumers may find and use them. These recommendations are applicable in general destination promotion terms and not restricted to food-related tourism initiatives. More fundamentally, however, the authors examine the way in which the structure of the institutional support systems for regional development and tourism destination marketing, in the UK, militates against the more effective "joining-up" of tourism-related development initiatives with tourism agencies' information provision networks.

The Isle of Arran Taste Trail, Scotland, UK

In Scotland, the *Isle of Arran Taste Trail* aims to promote Arran as a niche destination based on the quality of local catering and produce. The *Trail* is based around a guidebook that features participating businesses which grow, make or sell locally-produced beverages or foodstuffs. Additionally, the guidebook contains background information on the island's "natural larder" and recipes featuring local produce. The *Trail* web site *www.tastetrail.co.uk*, launched in January 2000, details the content of the guidebook with additional features such as recipe in-

FIGURE 2. The UK Case Study Areas

Source: authors

formation, hyperlinks to other food-related sites and travel information for visitors to the island–which includes direct external hyperlinks to the regional and national tourist board web sites.

While this initiative is acknowledged on the regional tourism authority's web site (*www.ayrshire-arran.com/*), and indeed this site does host a hyperlink to the *Taste Trail's* site, at the time of writing this paper, the hyperlink is "buried" on the *useful links* page of the web site under the heading "Useful Organizations." From a consumer's perspective, there is no mention of the *Taste Trail* under the *things to see and do* hyperlink–although several of the *Trail's* members are featured here. Clicking on the *search for . . . eating and drinking* hyperlink yields no success if one is searching for the *Taste Trail* as this hyperlink points the browser to the regional version of VisitScotland's national "eating and drinking database." Following the *Isle of Arran* hyperlink, the consumers will find themselves at a web page which lists a selection of itineraries, one of which is labelled "Food Trail." The *Food Trail* hyperlink takes the consumer to an Adobe Acrobat (.pdf) document which contains a one page description of five of the *Trail's* members (all food processors). Although this document does contain a reference to the *Taste Trail* in its description of one of these producers, this is not elaborated upon and there is no associated hyperlink to the *Taste Trail* web site.

Taste of the West Food Trails, England, UK

Taste of the West is the regional specialty food and drink group for the south west of England and provides economic development support for the food and drink industry throughout this area. *Taste of the West* is a limited company and receives government funding through the Food From Britain (FFB) agency. Their *Food Trails* initiative aims to support and enhance the regional food and drink industry by stimulating demand for their products. To achieve this, a collection of seven sub-regional guides containing information relating to these areas' food producers, processors and retailers and caterers as well as details of local farmers markets, recipes and travel information has been produced. These guides have been produced in both paper- and web-based formats.

The web-based *Food Trail* information can be found at *www.foodtrails. co.uk* from which it is possible to choose from the selection of individual guides (Cornwall, Dorset, Gloucestershire, North Devon, Somerset, South Devon and Wiltshire). Each of these localities has its own dedicated web site with internal hyperlinks to, and/or information on, businesses participating in the *Food Trail*. These participating businesses (members) are listed by sector–typically these sectors include bakery, dairy, fish, meat, preserves and snacks and retailers and eating places. Additionally, each area's web site features an interactive map which consumers can, using hyperlinks, browse for information on *Food Trail* members in any particular town or village. Each of the *Food Trail* web sites also contains external hyperlinks to a variety of local and regional tourist board web sites.

Once again, however, from a consumer's perspective, starting from the regional tourist board (South West Tourism) web *site–www.west countrynow.com*–the provision of hyperlinks to the *Food Trails* web site was found, largely, to be inadequate. The web-based tourism information provision for the South West Tourism region is structured in such a way that, from the *westcountrynow.com* web site, it is possible to select a particular locality by use of an interactive map. Having selected a locality, hyperlinks to a variety of locally-based web sites are displayed. Prominent amongst these is usually a local government-supported tourism information web site. However, among these, only a minority contain hyperlinks to the *Food Trails* web site, and in only one case is this link prominently displayed (*www.somewhere-special.co.uk*, created and maintained by South Hams District Council, South Devon). This dearth of hyperlinks to the *Food Trails* web site is despite the fact that, as with the *Isle of Arran Taste Trail*, each of the individual *Food Trails* web sites contain links to the respective local tourism information web site or web sites.

Towards Better Practice

Looking beyond the UK, one example of good practice in terms of providing online food-tourism related information for consumers is to be found at the Emilia Romagna Turismo web site (*www.emiliaromagnaturismo. it/index.asp*). From here, the web site's home page, a prominently displayed internal hyperlink directs browsers towards Emilia Romagna's *Le strade dei vini e dei sapori* (The wine and food routes), located in Central Northern Italy. From this page, it is possible to select from the nine sub-regional themed food- and wine-related trails. This is accomplished using an interactive map of the Emilia Romagna region containing internal and external hyperlinks to the individual themed food and wine routes. Alternatively, from the Emilia Romagna Turismo home page, it is possible to click an internal hyperlink to an English language version of the web site. The English language homepage, while not an exact facsimile of the Italian home page, does contain an internal hyperlink to *The wine and food routes* in the same prominent position as the Italian language version. Of the nine individual *routes*, three can be viewed in English and Italian–the remaining six can be viewed only in Italian.

Therefore, besides the commendable fact that the Emilia Romagna Turismo regional tourism information web site has a foreign (English) language option, it also contains a prominent hyperlink to guide consumers to the region's food-related tourism products–some of which can be viewed in English as well as Italian. It may be argued that the relative sophistication of this region's promotional material results from the longer history of development which gastronomic and food-related tourism initiatives have enjoyed in Italy in comparison with the UK. The degree of historical precedent is not, however, the only barrier which exists in the UK with regard to improving the provision of information in this respect.

The institutional support structure for regional tourism-related development in the UK is somewhat fragmented, insofar as enterprise networks (Local Enterprise Companies–LECs–in Scotland and Regional Development Agencies–RDAs–in England and Wales) are responsible for support for economic development while the remit for destination marketing lies with the network of national and regional tourist boards. A number of difficulties arise from this arrangement such as, for example, the lack of appropriate information on the tourist boards' web sites as described above. This would not be the case if the tourist boards themselves were stakeholders in the development initiatives. Elsewhere, anecdotal evidence has suggested that there are some cases where enterprise companies have been unwilling to lend financial development support to food-related initiatives on the basis that these contain a strong element of destination marketing–the remit for which lies not with the enterprise network, but with the tourist board network.

Other barriers which have become apparent during the course of this research relate: (i) to tourist boards' requirements for appropriate quality assurance systems to be in place before they will endorse any particular initiative; and (ii) in the case of *Taste of the West Food Trails* web sites, the presence of the external hyperlinks to the local tourism information web sites is largely in acknowledgement of the sponsorship which was received from these tourism organizations. While *Taste of the West* may wish to see reciprocal hyperlinks hosted on the tourism information web sites, the tourism organizations view the *Food Trails* initiative as just one of many tourism-related developments which are clamoring for the available space on their information web sites.

RECOMMENDATIONS FOR BEST PRACTICE

From an examination of the existing provision of web-based destination information relating to food-related tourism initiatives in the UK, this paper has highlighted that there is some way to go as regards improvements which could be made. While it is acknowledged that food trail-type initiatives are at an early stage of the product development cycle in the UK, and that the depth of relevant consumer research which would guide a more informed marketing philosophy approach to promotion is not at this time available, it is possible to develop, from this exploratory research, recommendations relating to the way in which web-based visitor information is provided. To assist with this the authors have constructed a theoretical taxonomy of consumers. This taxonomy classifies consumers according to the level of importance of food and gastronomy in their destination decision-making processes. We propose a four-fold taxonomy describing types of consumer as follows:

- for *Type I* consumers, gastronomy is an important element of their holiday experience and they actively seek information relating to an area's gastronomic heritage and/or the nature of the supply of locally-produced or quality food in the area;
- for *Type II* consumers, gastronomy is also important; however, they require exposure to the food-related tourism information as a precedent to acting upon this–that is, Type II consumers would not actively seek gastronomy-related information in a tourism context but welcome it, and may act upon it, when it is presented to them;
- *Type III* consumers do not attach importance to gastronomy as part of the holiday experience but may do so in the future if they have an enjoyable gastronomic experience-such as they may if knowledge of such opportunities is conferred to them and they go on to participate in some such activity during their tourism trip;
- finally, *Type IV* consumers have no interest in gastronomy and will continue to have no interest in gastronomy regardless of the quality or ubiquitousness of gastronomy-tourism promotional material.

This taxonomy is broadly supported by the findings described in MAFF/CA (2000, pp. 3-4) where holiday-makers in the UK, surveyed about their attitudes to regional and local foods, were segmented into five groups. These groups, ranked in descending order according to the importance of the contribution of regional and local foods to their holiday trips, were described as: food tourists; interested purchasers; the un-reached; the un-engaged; and laggards. The MAFF/CA report also found that the proportion of tourists purchasing or eating local foods during their visit was strongly related to their length of stay, noting that

"(T)his confirms opportunity is a key driver of purchase behavior" (p. 4). This finding supports the contention that, for Type II consumers in particular, but for the Types I and III also, exposure to local products is a key dimension in generating interest and sales. Before a consumer expresses *interest* in a product or service, however, their *attention* must be drawn to it. This paper now goes on to examine how best to achieve this in the context of web-based destination area promotion.

Location of Hyperlinks

As all consumers make use of the same tourist board web site, then the site design must cater for the lowest common denominator. Using the taxonomy presented above as an analytical framework, since Type IV consumers cannot be influenced, then the information provided must be suited at the very least to Type III consumers. Specifically, as these consumers will not actively search for gastronomy-related information on tourism information web sites, such information must therefore be provided in a conspicuous manner. From the web sites which have been viewed by the authors during the course of this research several approaches to providing food-related links have been noted. Figure 3 illustrates these approaches hierarchically, beginning with the most desirable and moving down to the least desirable.

In the case of Approach 4, a site search facility will work well for Type I consumers *provided that it works effectively*, that is, if the infor-

FIGURE 3. Approaches to Providing Hyperlinks

---

1. Direct external or internal hyperlink link from the tourism information provider's home page to the food-related tourism information web page, pages or site.

2. Internal hyperlink from the tourism information provider's home page to a "food and drink" or "eating and drinking" section of the web site–from here there is a direct external or internal hyperlink link to the food-related tourism information web page, pages or site.

3. Internal hyperlink from the tourism information provider's home page to an "itineraries," "things to see and do" or "activities" section of the web site–from here there is a direct external or internal hyperlink link to the food-related tourism information web page, pages or site.

4   Site search facility. This facility allows consumers to search the tourism information provider's web site for specific types of information. In our experience, this information seeking strategy does not often yield successful results. In particular, in some cases a search has resulted in no "hits" despite the fact that information relevant to the query is contained within the web site.

---

mation being sought exists on the web site, then it is found by the site search. The validity of these recommendations is not restricted to food-related tourism initiatives–they are potentially relevant in a wide variety of tourism information provision contexts. And the site search approach to information provision has been found wanting in several of these contexts. The problem seems to occur insofar as consumers will enter a somewhat specific search term–relating to the product or service that they are they are interested in–however, no "hits" are forthcoming as that particular term does not appear on the web site or, worse, it is there but there are technical limitations or difficulties with the search protocol. It is more productive to approach information provision from the opposite perspective whereby the consumer gradually moves towards the information they seek by navigating through a logical set of internal hyperlinks–unless of course, the web site is so extensive or poorly structured that such an approach is not feasible, in which case care must be taken to ensure technical adroitness in the associated search facility software.

CONCLUSION AND DISCUSSION

This paper is set against the background of ongoing food-related tourism development initiatives which, typically, draw upon regions' gastronomic heritage to strengthen the tourism product, enhance the visitor experience and help sustain local tourism, food production and processing sectors. In the UK, various regions are developing such food- and beverage-related tourism initiatives and some of these have developed a web-based presence. The underpinning rationale for the research is that, because such initiatives can generate a range of positive economic and social benefits, these should therefore be supported by effective promotional activities. It has been our experience, however, that, from a (potential) tourist's perspective, it can be difficult or even impossible to find hyperlinks from regional tourism information web sites to the food tourism initiatives' web sites.

Our analysis has found that, while food- and gastronomy-related tourism initiatives are at an early stage of the product development life cycle in the UK, there are other factors militating against the effective web-based promotion of such development initiatives. Firstly, the fragmented nature of the agencies responsible for supporting regional tourism development does not engender an integrated approach to product development and promotion–an approach which may be articulated within the marketing philosophy framework. Secondly, the way in which tourism information web sites are designed can have a critical bearing on the breadth of consumers who will find the relevant information. With regard to this latter point, we suggest an approach for positioning hyperlinks to food and drink initiatives in such a way as to cater to even those (potential) tourists who have no expressed interest in local or regional food and drink products or areas' gastronomic heritage. Although we do not explore these here, there are also design issues relating to consumers' technical and physical ability to access web-based information (see, for example, Byrne, 2001).

Concerning the infrastructure for regional tourism development in the UK: On the one hand, the Local Enterprise Companies, LECs (in Scotland), and Regional Development Agencies, RDAs (in England), are chiefly responsible for business support and development; while, on the other hand, destination information is provided variously by National and Area Tourist Boards and an array of Local Authority, local and regional organizations and local business consortia. This fragmentation between policy, planning and promotional support does little to engender the effective (web-based or otherwise) promotion of regional initiatives.

This failing can be argued to stem, at least in part, from the tourist boards lacking any ownership of these food tourism initiatives (there may also often be problems with issues such as initiatives' quality standards and status of participating businesses as regards tourist board membership). In Scotland, however, the recently published strategy document, *Tourism Framework for Action: 2002-2005* (Scottish Executive, 2002), may provide some impetus for a move towards the more effective joint working of the gamut of stakeholder agencies with roles to play in the coordinated development of a robust, sustainable and successful tourism sector. This impetus is rooted in the way that the *Framework for Action* places the onus of responsibility for achieving strategic goals directly with the agencies referred to above (and various others). Owing to the inter-sectoral nature of the tourism sector, it is perhaps not surprising that, in many cases, the Local Enterprise Companies (LECs) and the national (VisitScotland) and/or regional tourist boards (Area Tourist Boards) share responsibility for achieving development goals. It is further recommended, therefore, that, in the Scottish context, this opportunity is taken by policy makers to (more) clearly define: (a) the roles of the respective agencies; and (b) the organisational and communication structures which will enable them to work more effectively together.

REFERENCES

Bessière, J. (1998). Local development and heritage: Traditional food and cuisine as tourist attractions in rural areas. *Sociologia Ruralis*, 38 (1), 21-34.

Bessière, J. (2001). The role of gastronomy in tourism. In Roberts, L. & Hall, D. R. *Rural Tourism and Recreation: Principles to Practice*. Wallingford: CABI, 115-118.

Boyne, S., Williams, F. and Hall, D. R. (2001). Innovation in rural tourism and regional development: tourism and food production on the Isle of Arran. In Ruddy, J. & Flanagan, S. (eds). *ATLAS 10TH Anniversary International Conference Tourism Innovation and Regional Development*. Dublin Institute of Technology, Ireland, 4-6 October.

Boyne, S., Williams, F. & Hall, D. R. (2002). On the trail of regional success: Tourism, food production and the Isle of Arran Taste Trail. In Richards, G. & Hjalager, A-M. (eds). *Tourism and Gastronomy*. London: Routledge, 91-114.

Byrne, J. (2001). *Guidelines for Building an Accessible Web Site*. At <http://www.ispn.gcal.ac.uk/accsites/AccessGuide.html>. As viewed on 05/03/2002.

Choisy, C. (1996). Le poids du tourisme viti-vinicole (The significance of viticultural tourism). *Espaces*, 140, 30-33.

Clark, G., Darrall, J., Grove-White, R., Macnaghten, P. & Urry, J. (1994). Foreign marketing of the British countryside, *Leisure Landscapes. Leisure, culture and the English countryside: Challenges and conflicts. Background papers*. London: Council for the Protection of Rural England (CPRE), 160-170.

DCMS (Department of Media, Culture and Sport) (1999). *Tomorrow's Tourism*. London: DCMS.

DETR (Department of the Environment, Transport and the Regions) (2000). *Our Countryside: The future. A fair deal for rural England*. Norwich: HMSO.

ETC (English Tourism Council) (2001). *Working for the Countryside*. At <http://www.englishtourism.org.uk/downloads/policy/ruralSTRAT.pdf>. As viewed on 16/10/2001.

FFB (Food From Britain) (2002a). *Welcome to Food From Britain*. <http://www.foodfrombritain.com/>. As viewed on 28/03/2002.

FFB (Food from Britain) (2002b). *FFB's Specialty Food Service: Specialty Food Contacts*. <http://www.foodfrombritain.com/specialty_food_contacts.html>. As viewed on 28/03/2002.

Fields, K. (2002). Demand for the gastronomy tourism product: Motivational factors. In Richards, G. & Hjalager, A-M. (eds). *Tourism and Gastronomy*. London: Routledge, 36-50.

Hjalager, A-M. & Richards, G. (2002). Still undigested: Research issues in tourism and gastronomy. In Richards, G. & Hjalager, A-M. (eds). *Tourism and Gastronomy*. London: Routledge, 224-234.

Hudman, L. E. (1986). The travellers' perceptions of the role of food in the tourist industry. In *The impact of catering and cuisine upon tourism*. Proceedings of the 36th Congress of the International Association of Scientific Experts of Tourism (AIEST). 31 August to 6 September, Montreux, Switzerland.

Hughes, G. (1995a). Authenticity in tourism. *Annals of Tourism Research*, 22 (4), 781-803.

Hughes, G. (1995b). Food, tourism and Scottish heritage. In Leslie, D. (ed.). *Tourism and leisure: Towards the millennium. Volume 1: Tourism and leisure-culture, heritage and participation.* Eastbourne: Leisure Studies Association, 109-120.

Kneafsey, M. and Ilbery, B. (2001). Regional images and the promotion of specialty food and drink in the West Country. *Geography,* 86 (2), 131-140.

Kristula, D. (2002a). *What is the Internet?. At <http://www.davesite.com/webstation/inet101/net01.shtml>. As viewed on 15/04/2002.*

Kristula, D. (2002b). *What is the World Wide Web?.* At <http://www.davesite.com/webstation/inet101/www01.shtml>. As viewed on 15/04/2002.

Kuznesof, S., Tregear, A. & Moxey, A. (1997). Regional foods: A consumer perspective. *British Food Journal,* 99 (6), 199-206.

Law, R. (2000). Internet in travel and tourism. *Journal of Travel and Tourism Marketing,* 9 (3), 65-71.

MAFF/CA (Ministry of Agriculture, Fisheries and Food/Countryside Agency) (2000). *Tourists' attitudes towards regional and local foods.* London: MAFF. Available online at <http://www.defra.gov.uk/foodrin/helpmark/report.pdf>. As viewed on 25/04/2002.

Marris, T. (1986). Does food matter. *The Tourist Review,* 41 (4), 17-20.

Mitchell, R., Hall, C. M. & McIntosh, A. (2000). Wine tourism and consumer behavior. In Hall, C. M., Sharples, L., Cambourne, B. & Macionis, N. (eds). *Wine Tourism Around the World: Development, Management and Markets.* (pp. 115-135). Oxford: Butterworth-Heinemann.

Richards, G. & Hjalager, A-M. (eds) (2002). *Tourism and Gastronomy.* London: Routledge.

Scarpato, R. (2002). Sustainable gastronomy as a tourist product. In Richards, G. & Hjalager, A-M. (eds). *Tourism and gastronomy.* (pp. 51-70). London: Routledge.

Scottish Executive (2001). *A Forward Strategy for Scottish Agriculture.* Edinburgh: Scottish Executive.

Scottish Executive (2002). *Tourism Framework for Action: 2002-2005.* Edinburgh: Scottish Executive.

Skaggs, R., Falk, C., Almonte, J. & Cárdenas, M. (1996). Product-country images and international food marketing: Relationships and research needs. *Agribusiness,* 12, 593-600.

Smith, M. (2002). *Weaving the web to attract tourists. The Herald* 06/02/2002. <http://www.theherald.co.uk/>. As viewed 06/02/2002.

Sørensen, A. & Nilsson, P. Å. (2000). Virtual rurality versus rural reality–contemplating the attraction of the rural. In K. O. K. Olsen & N. K. Prebensen (eds). *Hovedforedrag og papers fra det 8. Nordiske Forskersymposium i Turisme* (pp. 379-392). Alta, Norway: Høgskolen i Finnmark.

Symons, M. (1999). Gastronomic authenticity and sense of place. In *Proceedings of Ninth CAUTHE National Research Conference.* Adelaide: CAUTHE, 333-340.

Telfer, D. J. (2000). Tastes of Niagara: Building strategic alliances between tourism and agriculture. *International Journal of Hospitality and Tourism Administration,* 1 (1), 71-88.

Telfer, D. J. & Wall, G. (1996). Linkages between tourism and food production. *Annals of Tourism Research,* 23(3), 635-653.

Tregear, A., Kuznesof, S. & Moxey, A. (1998). Policy initiatives for regional foods: some insights from consumer research. *Food Policy*, 23 (5) 383-394.

van Westering, J. (1999). Heritage and gastronomy: the pursuits of the 'new tourist.' *International Journal of Heritage Studies*, 5 (2), 75-81.

Wan, C.-S. (2002). The web sites of international tourist hotels and tour wholesalers in Taiwan. *Tourism Management*, 23 (2), 155-160.

APPENDIX 1

Web Sites Referred to in the Paper

Organisation	Web site location
Ayrshire and Arran Tourist Board (Scotland, UK)	http://www.ayrshire-arran.com
Emilia Romagna Turismo (Italy)	http://www.emiliaromagnaturismo.it/index.asp
Isle of Arran Taste Trail (Scotland, UK)	http://www.tastetrail.co.uk
South Hams (of South Devon) District Council Tourism Information Web Site (England, UK)	http://www.somewhere-special.co.uk
South West Tourism (England, UK)	http://www.westcountrynow.com
Taste of the West Foodtrails (England, UK)	http://www.foodtrails.co.uk
VisitScotland (Scotland, UK)	http://www.visitscotland.com/

Seasonality in New Zealand
Winery Visitation:
An Issue of Demand and Supply

Richard D. Mitchell
C. Michael Hall

SUMMARY. Seasonality is a major issue in tourism management; however, the implications of seasonality for wine tourism have only received limited attention. Arguably, because of the interaction between seasonal patterns of consumer demand with the inherent seasonality of vineyard work and wine supply means that seasonality issues may be even more problematic for wine tourism than other forms of tourism. The article provides the results of a national study on wine tourism in New Zealand. The article highlights the seasonal nature of visitation and suggests a number of marketing strategies by which some of the effects of seasonality may be overcome in terms of both target markets and the improved management of human resources. *[Article copies available for a fee from The Haworth Document Delivery Service: 1-800-HAWORTH. E-mail address: <docdelivery@haworthpress.com> Website: <http://www.HaworthPress.com> © 2003 by The Haworth Press, Inc. All rights reserved.]*

Richard D. Mitchell is Senior Lecturer in Tourism, Department of Tourism, School of Business, University of Otago, Dunedin, New Zealand (E-mail: RDMitchell@business.ac.nz). C. Michael Hall is Professor and Head of Department, Centre for Tourism, University of Otago, Dunedin, New Zealand (E-mail: cmhall@business.otago.ac.nz).

[Haworth co-indexing entry note]: "Seasonality in New Zealand Winery Visitation: An Issue of Demand and Supply." Mitchell, Richard D., and C. Michael Hall. Co-published simultaneously in *Journal of Travel & Tourism Marketing* (The Haworth Hospitality Press, an imprint of The Haworth Press, Inc.) Vol. 14, No. 3/4, 2003, pp. 155-173; and: *Wine, Food, and Tourism Marketing* (ed: C. Michael Hall) The Haworth Hospitality Press, an imprint of The Haworth Press, Inc., 2003, pp. 155-173. Single or multiple copies of this article are available for a fee from The Haworth Document Delivery Service [1-800-HAWORTH, 9:00 a.m. - 5:00 p.m. (EST). E-mail address: docdelivery@haworthpress.com].

http://www.haworthpress.com/store/product.asp?sku=J073
© 2003 by The Haworth Press, Inc. All rights reserved.
10.1300/J073v14n03_09

KEYWORDS. Wine tourism, seasonality, New Zealand

INTRODUCTION

Seasonal fluctuations in the demand for and supply of attractions and destinations are endemic within the tourism industry and Hinch and Jackson (2000, p. 87) suggest that ". . . paradoxically, it is also one of the least understood." Seasonality is not confined to tourism, with industries such as agriculture also being heavily influenced by seasonal variations in production and consumption (Cooper, Fletcher, Gilbert & Wanhill, 1993). Therefore tourism sectors such as wine tourism–a confluence of these two highly seasonal industries–are likely to have significant issues to overcome in relation to the management and marketing of their products (Getz, 2000).

This article explores seasonality in New Zealand wine tourism, providing an analysis of the seasonal preferences for visitation, estimates of the actual demand and variation between several segments of the wine tourism market. It also attempts to explain some of the reasons for the visitation patterns and proposes a model of the supply and demand influences on winery visitation seasonality.

TOURISM, WINE TOURISM AND SEASONALITY

Tourism seasonality has been an important issue in tourism literature since Bar-On published his text *Seasonality in Tourism* (Hinch & Jackson, 2000). More recently, seasonality has been revisited by a number of authors (in particular *Seasonality in Tourism* edited by Baum and Lundtorp, 2001a), many of whom have lamented at the lack of progress in our understanding of the causes of the phenomenon (e.g., Baum & Lundtorp, 2001b; Butler, 2001; Hinch and Jackson, 2000). Butler (2001) identifies several main forms or causes of tourism seasonality. These include:

- Natural (e.g., climate, especially in high latitudes).
- Institutionalized (e.g., school or public holidays).
- Social pressure or fashion (e.g., privileged elite's seasonal participation in recreation activities and mass following class such as bird or deer hunting).
- Sporting season (e.g., winter and skiing and summer and surfing).
- Inertia or tradition (e.g., continuing to take vacations during school holiday periods even when children have left school).

Butler (2001) also provides a model of the influences on tourism seasonality that includes "demand factors" (e.g., response to natural seasons, institutionalized holidays, etc), "supply factors" (e.g., climate, physical attractions, etc.) and "modifying actions" (differential pricing, market diversification, etc.), whose interaction manifests in patterns of tourism seasonality at a destination.

All of these causes of seasonality can have an impact on winery visitation; however, it is the "natural" influence that most obviously impacts on both the supply of and demand for wine tourism. A number of authors have hinted at this (e.g., Getz, 2000; Johnson, 1998). Further, Getz (2000: 10) suggests that ". . . wine tourism presents many opportunities for attracting visitors year round [and] these stem in part from the inherent seasonality of the viniculture process." He provides a list of seasonal activities that occur on the vineyard and in the winery that provide opportunities for the development of tourism products (e.g., bud burst in spring, grapes on vines in summer, harvest in autumn and ice wine production in winter). King (2000) also suggests that wine tourism is less seasonal than other forms of tourism. However, this assumption is based on Maddern and Golledge's (1996) finding that 56 percent of Victorian wine tourists prefer to visit any time of year, rather than any measure of fluctuating visitation throughout the year.

Therefore there is an apparent paradox within the literature, in that the seasonal nature of wine production and tourism is not necessarily manifest in high seasonal in winery visitation. However, to date, little or no empirical evidence has been published relating to this phenomenon and there has been no explanation of seasonal patterns of winery visitation.

A number of the studies of winery visitors have been completed in the last decade; however, only a relatively small number have attempted to explore general winery visitation behaviour such as seasonal preferences. Measures of general winery visitation have usually been limited to an estimate of the value of purchases made at wineries (e.g., Beverland, James, James, Porter and Stace, 1998a, b; Dodd, 1995, Dodd and Bigotte, 1995, 1997; Jackson, 2000; Longo, 1999; Machin, 2000; Morris and King, 1997) or the number of visits that an individual made to wineries in the previous 12 months (e.g., Jackson, 2000; Longo, 1999; Maddern and Golledge, 1996). Meanwhile a few studies have provided insights into other aspects of generally winery visitation behaviour, including the timing of the previous visit (Longo, 1999; Maddern and Golledge, 1996) and the time of the year that visitors prefer to visit (Maddern and Golledge, 1996). It is clear from an analysis of the demand-side literature on winery visitation, then, that the most significant gap that exists is in the area seasonal variations in visitation (refer Table 1).

Maddern and Golledge (1996) provide one of the most in-depth analyses of general winery visitation behavior (Victoria, Australia), including data on the preferred time of the year for visitation. However the data collected provided little detail on seasonality, as more than half of the respondents (56 percent) stated that they preferred to visit *"any time of the year."*

While no published demand-side studies exist in this area, data collected by Johnson (1998) provides an insight into supply-side estimates of New Zealand winery visitation. Figure 1 shows that the summer months of December, January and February see the highest numbers of visitors (all above 350,000 visits for the month), while May to September see less than 200,000 visitors per month. These data make comparison possible with the monthly preferences identified in the current study.

THE NEW ZEALAND WINERY VISITORS' SURVEY

A convenience sample of 33 wineries distributed approximately 3,000 questionnaires to visitors to nine of New Zealand's wine regions. Each winery was asked to randomly distribute 100 questionnaires over a ten-week period beginning late January 1999. Of the approximately 3,000 questionnaires distributed, 1,104 were returned (representing a

TABLE 1. Comparisons of General Winery Behaviour Profiles

	One to five Visits/year %	Visited in last 6 months %	Prefer summer visits %	Average wine purchase $1-$50 %
New Zealand Winery Visitors' Survey	**57.3**	**58.7[1]**	**50.7**	**52.7**
Texas	25[2]	-	-	[3]
Victoria	67	52	[3]	-
Augusta-Margaret River	-	-	-	25
Tasmania	81[4]	-	-	[3]
New Zealand (Longo)	79[5]	50	-	-

Sources: *Texas Wineries* = Dodd (1995); Dodd and Bigotte (1995, 1997); *Victorian Wineries* = Maddern and Golledge (1996); *Augusta-Margaret River Wineries* = Morris and King (1997); *Tasmanian Wineries* = Jackson (2000); *New Zealand Wineries* = Longo (1999).
Notes: 1 = those that visited another winery in the region. Those that visited another New Zealand winery outside the region in the last six months totaled 57.7 percent, the winery where the survey was completed 52.0 percent and a winery overseas 16.0 percent. 2 = those visiting other wineries in Texas in the previous 12 months. Total number of previous visits to the winery of survey between one and five totaled 23 percent. 3 = a measure was taken but the results are not directly comparable with the NZWVS. 4 = average number of visits per year to any winery in Australia by Tasmanian winery visitors. 5 = the total number of previous visits, not just the number in the last 12 months.

FIGURE 1. Johnson's (1998) Estimated Average Monthly Visitation to New Zealand Wineries

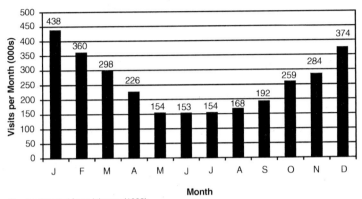

Source: Adapted from Johnson (1998).

response rate of approximately 37%). Fourteen questionnaires returned were unusable, resulting in a total usable sample of 1,090.

Many of the questions used in the survey were adapted from those of other surveys of winery visitors. In particular, a number of questions were drawn or adapted from studies in Victoria, Australia (Maddern and Golledge, 1996) and Texas, USA (Dodd and Bigotte, 1995), to allow for a degree of comparison with other countries. Additional questions were included to further explore the regional and temporal context of the winery visit.

This article explores the questions asked in a section entitled *Previous Winery Visits*. In this section, respondents were asked (amongst other things) *what months of the year they MOST prefer to visit wineries* and they were able to select as many months as the wished. A number of segmentation criteria have also been used in order to further understand the behaviour exhibited. Segmentation was carried out on the basis of findings from an analysis of the demographics of respondents to the survey and the literature pertaining to winery visitation and the general wine market (refer to Table 2).

DEMAND SEASONALITY
IN NEW ZEALAND WINERY VISITATION

Late summer/early autumn was the most preferred time of the year to visit, with January, February and March the three most popular months

TABLE 2. Bases for Segmentation Criteria

	Region	Country of origin	Gender	Generation	Wine Knowledge
Winery Visitors					
Beverland (1999)	-	√	-	√	√
Beverland et al. (1998a, b)	-	√	-	-	√
Longo (1999)	-	√	√	-	√
Machin (2000)	-	√	√	-	√
Maddern and Golledge (1996)	√	√	√	-	√
Morris and King (1997)	-	√	√	-	√
O'Neill and Charters (1999, 2000)	√	√	√	-	-
General Wine Market					
Batt and Dean (2000)	-	-	√	-	-
Cartiere (1997)	-	-	√	√	-
Keown and Casey (1994)	-	-	√	-	-
Koerber (2000)	-	-	-	√	-
Murphy (1999)	-	-	-	√	-
Sansoni (1998)	-	-	-	√	-
Scarpa (1999)	-	-	-	√	-
Stanford (2000)	-	-	√	-	-

(13.1 percent, 18.3 percent and 16.6 percent of responses, respectively). November through January was also popular, while May to August were the least preferred months (refer to Figure 2). The warmer months are clearly the most preferred time of the year to visit a winery, reflecting both the importance of outdoor elements associated with visiting a winery (e.g., al fresco dining, scenery and vineyard ambience) and the fact that wineries are less likely to be open to the public during the months where the vineyard lies dormant or when harvest activity is high (Johnson 1999).

Further, a comparison with Johnson's (1999) estimate suggests seasonality in preferences is greater than the pattern of estimated monthly visitation (refer to Figure 3). It should be noted, however, that some caution must be taken in interpreting these data as some sampling bias towards January to March may have been experienced as the survey was undertaken between 30 January and 16 April 1999.

Wine Region

While the multiple response nature of the data did not permit any test for statistical significance, an examination of a regional breakdown of

FIGURE 2. Preferred Time of Year to Visit Wineries (n = 3,101)

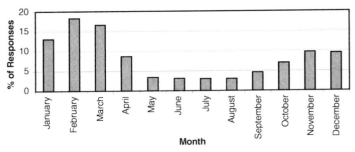

Note: < N because respondents were able to select more than one month.

FIGURE 3. Comparison with Johnson's 1998 Estimate of New Zealand Winery Visitation

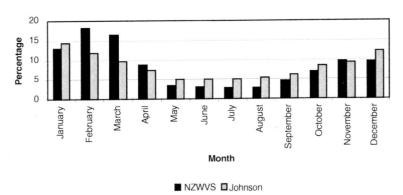

■ NZWVS □ Johnson

the data on preferred time of the year reveals that there was little variation in those preferring to visit during summer (refer to Table 3). Some
variation was observed amongst spring preferences, but these tended to
lie at the extremes (for example, Auckland at 31.1 percent compared
with Nelson at 18.9 percent), with most regions clustered around the
mean.

Considerable regional variation was observed between respondents
preferring to visit in both autumn and winter. Autumn preferences
ranged from to almost half of the respondents (47.4 percent in
Auckland) to little more than one in five respondents (21.9 percent in
Bay of Plenty). While the popularity of winter visits remained low
across all regions, this ranged from almost one in five Auckland respon-

TABLE 3. Regional, Winery Category and Country of Origin Preferred Time of Year to Visit Wineries

Season	Summer†	Autumn†	Winter†	Spring†
All New Zealand (n = 883)	50.7%	35.6%	11.4%	26.4%
Regions				
Auckland (n = 76)	48.7%	47.4%	18.9%	31.1%
Bay of Plenty (n = 38)	54.4%	21.9%	6.1%	21.9%
Hawkes Bay (n = 114)	47.4%	36.3%	8.8%	21.9%
Northland (n = 17)	52.9%	27.5%	11.8%	23.5%
Wairarapa (n = 55)	58.8%	29.7%	6.1%	29.1%
Canterbury* (n = 8)	70.8%	29.2%	8.3%	20.8%
Central Otago (n = 269)	51.4%	33.5%	11.3%	27.1%
Marlborough (n = 175)	48.6%	38.5%	14.9%	30.3%
Nelson (n = 81)	49.8%	37.4%	7.0%	18.9%
Country of Origin				
New Zealand (n = 707)	54.3%	36.5%	9.5%	26.9%
Overseas (n = 104)	24.4%	29.5%	23.4%	23.4%

Note: Numbers are percentage of respondents and totals add to more than 100 percent as respondents were able to choose more than one month.
*There are only 8 individuals in the Canterbury sample, therefore these figures should be viewed with caution.
† Southern hemisphere seasons only. Data not adjusted for seasonal differences for the respondents that reside in northern hemisphere countries.

dents (18.9 percent) to as few as 6.1 percent for Bay of Plenty and Wairarapa respondents. In the main, respondents from those regions that are popular domestic summer resorts (i.e., Bay of Plenty, Wairarapa, Nelson and Hawkes Bay) were least likely to prefer a winter visit, reflecting normal patterns of tourism seasonality for the regions.

Both Auckland and Marlborough exhibited least seasonal variation. For Marlborough, this may be due to the fact that the region is largely a wine destination and therefore winery visitation is likely to be important across all seasons. Auckland, on the hand, is located on the urban fringe and is dominated by a local market (e.g., Mitchell and Hall, 2001a) that is more likely to make multiple visits during the year, thus reducing the seasonal effect.

Preferred Season for Winery Visitation versus Tourist Arrivals

A comparison between seasonal fluctuations in preferred winery visitation and regional tourism statistics (1998/1999 guest nights) provides a useful basis for discussion on this phenomenon. Figure 4 shows that,

FIGURE 4. Preferred Winery Visitation and Guest Night Seasonality (June 1998-May 1999)

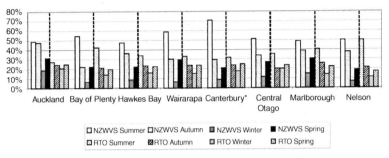

Note: Data is not available for Tourism Northland until February 1999.
RTO = Regional Tourism Organisation for the wine region (i.e., Tourism Auckland, Tourism Bay of Plenty, Tourism Hawke's Bay, Tourism Wairarapa, Chistchurch & Canterbury Marketing, Destination Queenstown, Destination Marlborough and Latitude Nelson).
*Canterbury has only 8 respondents therefore these figures should be viewed with caution.
Note: RTO rows do not add to 100 as the percentage is that for the calendar year, not the 12 months shown.

in general, winery visitation reflects peaks and troughs in tourist activity, with summer the high season for general tourist numbers and preferred winery visitation across all regions. Further, there is evidence that the combination of agricultural and tourism activities results on a compounded seasonal effect, with winery visitation more seasonally variable than general tourist activity (especially Bay of Plenty, Hawkes Bay and Wairarapa).

Despite some evidence of a correlation between general tourist activity and visitation (i.e., peaks and troughs in proportion with each other), there are a number of regions that exhibit inconsistencies in this area. Wairarapa wineries, for example, exhibited a large differentiation between preferred summer and winter visitation, while general tourist activity was much less seasonal. This is perhaps reflective of the fact that many of the winery visitors to the region were likely to be on a day trip from Wellington and the figures used to measure tourist activity are based on overnight stays. On the other hand, Central Otago tourist activity, while exhibiting a high season in summer, also has strong winter tourist activity–a manifestation of a strong local ski industry. However, Central Otago winery visitors (11.3 percent) were no more likely than the overall sample (11.4 percent) to prefer winter visits. Further, Auckland wineries have a low level of seasonality in accordance with a relatively even spread of tourist activity throughout the year. However, the vast majority of visitors to Auckland wineries were from the

Auckland region (Mitchell and Hall, 2001a) and therefore little can be made of the correlation between tourist activity and winery visitation in the region. Therefore, the explanation of winery visitation seasonality is not simply a function of the regional tourism activity and a more detailed examination of demand and supply seasonality is necessary.

Country of Origin

While preferred visitation patterns of New Zealand respondents closely resembled that of the whole sample, there was very little seasonal preference for international visitors. This remains true even when statistics are adjusted to account for respondents from northern hemisphere countries, where seasons correspond to different months (adjusted for hemisphere: 27.6% summer; 25.6% autumn; 20.2 winter; 27.2 spring) (refer to Table 3).

Level of commitment and interest may, at least in part, explain the less seasonal nature of the international market. It can be assumed that the international respondents have made a considerable investment in both time and money to visit a winery in New Zealand and therefore are more likely to be more wine interested/committed than their New Zealand counterparts. This assumption is supported by discussion by pertaining to a range of indicators of the wine interest of winery visitors in New Zealand (Mitchell & Hall, 2001b) and Australia (Maddern & Golledge, 1996). Wine interest and commitment is significant because those with a higher degree of commitment to wine are more likely to visit wineries year round (for example see the discussion later relating to wine knowledge–a measure of interest in commitment).

Generation

A generational breakdown of these data shows that preferences for visiting in summer decreased with age (refer toFigure 5). Generation Y and X, in particular, demonstrated a slightly higher preference for summer visits than all other generations (59.0 percent and 57.5 percent compared with 47.1 percent for Baby Boomers, the next highest). However, preferences for visiting during the winter months increased with age, doubling from 7.7 percent for Generation Y to 14.9 percent for Seniors. Baby Boomers had the greatest preference for visits during both shoulder seasons. Figure 5 shows that Baby Boomers also had a wider range of preferences than the other generations.

FIGURE 5. Generational Breakdown of Preferred Time of Year to Visit Wineries

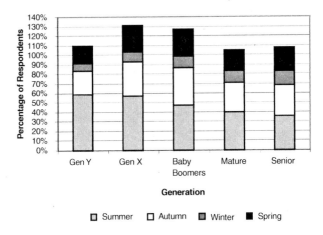

Some explanation for these preferences might be found by exploring the relationship between generation and wine interest. Baby Boomers, for example, have the highest level of wine interest and, as such, are more likely to make a wider range of choices about when and where to visit. On the other hand, Generation Y and X respondents were less wine interested and knowledgeable and were most likely to focus on visiting during peak seasons.

Wine Knowledge

Figure 6 shows that the range of preferences increases with level of knowledge. In particular, while around 50 percent of respondents at each level of knowledge indicated that they preferred to visit during the summer months, preferences for all other seasons increase with level of knowledge (for the winter months, each level of knowledge 1.5 times that of the previous). Therefore, increased wine knowledge increased the propensity to visit during shoulder-seasons and, more particularly, off-seasons. This is further evidence that level of wine knowledge is an indicator of commitment to wine, wine-related behavior and wine tourism activity and supports the assertions made relating to country of origin and generation.

Mitchell and Hall (2001b) suggest that several of the behavior differences associated with level of wine knowledge (in particular those asso-

FIGURE 6. Wine Knowledge Breakdown of Preferred Time of Year to Visit Wineries

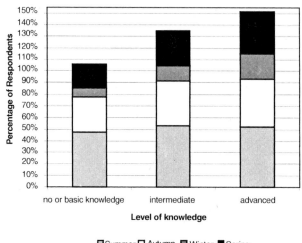

ciated with place of purchase) might be attributed to the greater propensity for neophilic behavior amongst those with high levels of knowledge (see also Dodd, 1997). The concept of neophilia is also instrumental in the explanation of the winery visitation behaviors observed above. The desire for new experiences and new tastes, for example, is likely to drive those with a high level of knowledge to visit wineries throughout the year in order to taste new vintages the moment they are released and to make purchases across the range of wines produced (reflected in a higher level of reported purchases at wineries).

SUPPLY SEASONALITY IN NEW ZEALAND WINE TOURISM

While demand influences are an important component of wine tourism seasonality, this is only part of the explanation for the patterns of winery visitation. A number of supply-side issues also have a significant impact on the timing of visits to wineries.

Resourcing Dilemma

Cooper et al. (1993), suggest that a "striking feature" of tourism *and* agriculture is that they are both subject to seasonal variations in activity, insinuating that businesses which combine both agriculture and tourism are likely to have compounded seasonal effects. Cooper et al. (1993, p. 132) continue that "any business subject to seasonal variations in demand for its output is faced with a dilemma." The dilemma is whether to resource the business to cope with peak demand and output (and therefore over resource for much of the year) or to estimate average demand and try to cope with periods of high demand. This is especially significant for New Zealand wineries, where 93% of wineries are small producers (New Zealand Winegrowers, 2002) and therefore have less capacity to manage the limited resources available to them. One of the strategies employed to minimize resourcing conflicts, whether by design or not, is for wineries to reduce the emphasis on the cellar door at times of high vineyard and winery activity and to increase it during low activity.

The Progress of Nature

The progress of nature in the vineyard is also an important consideration, as it has significant implications for resources and has a strong correlation with the preferences for visiting. This latter point is reflective of the vineyard setting as an important attraction for visitors (i.e., al fresco dining and the setting and scenery associated with winery visits), which is at its most appealing phase during summer (e.g., vines in full bloom) and early autumn (e.g., colored foliage). Johnson (1999: 70) suggests that:

> *Opening times for wineries . . . reflect the progress of nature. During the winter months vines become dormant and bereft of leaves, bud burst occurs in late spring and flowering in November-December (New Zealand Geographic and Montana Wines 1997). Grapes grow over the summer months to be harvested in autumn (as early as March and as late as May, and even into June in Otago). Opening times tend to be longer when vines are active or grapes are harvested. Opening hours are at their peak during the summer months when grapes are developing on the vine.*

As a result of the progress of nature, the harvest months, perhaps the shoulder season with the greatest of Getz's (2000) opportunities to develop wine tourism products (e.g., harvest festivals, wine making demonstrations and simply the most interesting time to visit for those interested to learn more about wine making), also have the highest demand on a winery's resources. Perhaps a little surprisingly, the winter months, the time of the year with the lowest demand on resources, also present few opportunities for expansion of visitation. Not only is the vineyard bare and winery activity low, but many winemakers and vitculturalists take the opportunity to expand their skills and knowledge by travelling to a northern hemisphere winery to work on a vintage, while seasonal labor (both from the wine industry and tourism and hospitality sector) moves to regions and centres where other seasonal work is available. This leaves human resources at a premium and the ability to minimize seasonal troughs is reduced. In New Zealand a possible exception to this is Central Otago, where a strong winter tourist season, based on the local ski industry, might provide the necessary demand and strong local labor market for expansion of off-season services. To date, however, demand for winter visitation in this region appears to be light, once again reflecting the unattractiveness of vineyards and wineries during the winter months.

Other Outlets for Wine Sales

While many wineries see cellar door operations as an important part of their business function (Johnson's (1998) finding that 75 percent of New Zealand wineries rated the cellar door as extremely or very important to sales), this is just one outlet for the wine that they produce. The most popular place of purchase amongst New Zealand winery visitors is the supermarket (Mitchell & Hall, 2001b), but wineries also distribute their wine through retail wine and liquor stores, restaurants, wholesalers and export markets. As a result Johnson (1998) found that the cellar door sales accounted for an average of just 20 percent of revenue for New Zealand wineries, but this was as little as 9 percent or as much as 37 percent, depending on the region of the winery.

Further, New Zealand wineries have been reluctant to invest in tourism-related infrastructure, despite recognizing its importance (Hall et. al., 2000). Hall et al. (2000, p. 157) suggest that the reasons for this are several-fold but stress that it is clearly related to the opportunity costs of spending scarce time and money on cellar door facilities at the expense of ". . . developing more traditional distribution channels and production expansion that may also lead to greater sales in the future." As a result of this attitude toward cellar door investment and the focus on other distribution channels winery owners have little motivation to mitigate the adverse effects of seasonal variations in cellar door visitation.

CONCLUSION:
A MODEL OF WINERY VISITATION SEASONALITY

Winery visitation in New Zealand is highly seasonal both in terms of market preference, estimated visitation and supply of the wine tourism product. While Getz (2000) suggests that the "inherent seasonality" of viticulture allows for product development and marketing opportunities, the complex interaction between supply and demand seasonality limits the ability of many wineries to take advantage of such opportunities. Butler (2001) acknowledges the influence of both supply and demand factors on patterns of tourism seasonality and this article has identified a range of wine tourism supply and demand influences on winery visitation seasonality. Figure 7 illustrates the complex relationship between these elements, hinting at the compound effect of highly

FIGURE 7. Supply and Demand Influences on Winery Visitation Seasonality in New Zealand

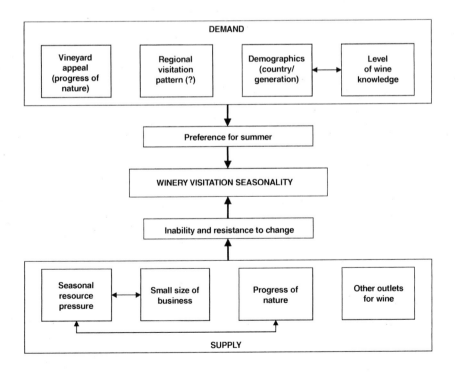

seasonal preferences for summer and an inability or reluctance of the industry to mitigate the adverse effects of seasonality.

In terms of demand, a strong preference for summer is also manifest in estimates of visitation made by the New Zealand wine industry. However, seasonal preferences are influenced by a number of aspects of the market (e.g., country of origin, generation and especially level of wine knowledge), the wine region (e.g., existing tourist traffic and the nature of its general tourist market) and the progress of nature (e.g., the varying appeal of the vineyard setting and winery activity throughout the year). In previous work by the current authors a relationship has also been established between demographic characteristics and wine knowledge, further complicating the influence on wine and winery related behavior (e.g., Mitchell & Hall, 2001b). Moreover, some inconsistencies were observed in the relationship between general tourist activity and winery visitation, suggesting that the winery visitors do not necessarily have the same patterns of behavior as the general tourist population for a region.

From a supply perspective, a winery's ability to minimise cellar door seasonality is influenced by an inability and/or reluctance to change the way they deliver cellar door services. In particular, the interaction between the progress of nature (e.g., seasonal demands on the resources of the winery), the small size of around 93 percent of New Zealand wine producers and other seasonal demands on resources (e.g., winemakers and viticulturalists taking part in northern hemisphere vintages). Wineries also have a number of options available to them for the sale and distribution of their wine, which lessens the impact of seasonal variations in cellar door visitation on both the cash flow and bottom line of the winery.

The implications for wineries are several-fold (e.g., the resourcing dilemma, cash flow and budgetary planning) and are dependent on a number of factors (e.g., the resources available, general tourist traffic in the region, the target market of winery, etc.). However, perhaps the most important issue is the answer to the question, does seasonal variation in cellar door visitation have an adverse impact on the winery's business? The answer depends largely on the emphasis that an individual winery places on the cellar door as a sales outlet. The average income from cellar door operation is low across New Zealand (just 20 percent), but some wineries rely heavily on cellar door sales for income. This is especially true of wineries in the early stages of establishing a presence in the market place, those with limited access to the traditional distribution channels (e.g., those from emerging regions may find it hard to establish relationships with distributors, restaurants and retailers) (Johnson, 1998) and/or those with limited resources to undertake their own marketing and sales activities. In these instances seasonality in visitation will have a substantial impact on the winery's viability and the impact is compounded by the fact that these wineries are usually the least able to cope with peaks and troughs cash flow. The impacts are also significant for wine regions that rely heavily on wine tourism to attract visitors, although evidence from the current study suggests that preferences to visit such regions (e.g., Marlborough) are a little less seasonal than other regions. In order to minimise the impacts of seasonality wineries and wine regions need to both target markets that are less seasonal in their preferences (e.g., those with a high level of wine knowledge and Baby Boomers) and identify ways to more effectively manage the human resources available to them. This will require a strong understanding of their market and its demands, as well as recognising the limitations and strengths of their resource base.

REFERENCES

Batt, P. J. & Dean, A. (2000). Factors that influence consumer's decisions. *Australian and New Zealand Wine Industry Journal: First International Wine Marketing Supplement, 15*(4): 34-41.

Baum, T. & Lundtorp, S. (eds.) (2001a). *Seasonality in Tourism.* Oxford: Pergamon/Elsevier Science.

Baum, T. & Lundtorp, S. (2001b). Introduction. In Baum, T. and Lundtorp, S. (eds.) *Sesasonality in Tourism.* (pp. 1-4) Oxford: Pergamon/Elsevier Science.

Beverland, M. (1999). Old World vs. New in wine tourism and marketing? *Australian and New Zealand Wine Industry Journal, 14*(6): 95-100.

Beverland, M., James, K., James, M., Porter, C. & Stace, G. (1998a). Wine tourists–a missed opportunity or a misplaced priority? In J. Kandampully (ed.) *Advances in Research, New Zealand Tourism and Hospitality Conference Proceedings.* Lincoln: Lincoln University.

Beverland, M., James, K., James, M., Porter, C. & Stace, G. (1998b). Wine tourists–missed opportunities in West Auckland. *Australian and New Zealand Wine Industry Journal, 13*(4): 403-407.

Butler, R. W. (2001). Seasonality in Tourism. In Baum, T. & Lundtorp, S. (eds.) *Sesasonality in Tourism.* Oxford: Pergamon/Elsevier Science, 5-22.

Cartiere, R. (1997). Concern over 'typical' wine drinker: After aging baby boomers, who is the next generation? *Wine Business Monthly,* July [online edition]

Cooper, C., Fletcher, J., Gilbert, D. & Wanhill, S. (1993). *Tourism: Principles and Practice.* Harlow: Longman.

Dodd, T. H. (1995). Opportunities and pitfalls of tourism in a developing wine industry. *International Journal of Wine Marketing, 7*(1): 5-16.

Dodd, T. H. and V. Bigotte (1995). *Visitors to Texas Wineries: Their Demographic Characteristics and Purchasing Behavior.* Texas: Texas Wine Marketing Research Institute.

Dodd, T. H. and V. Bigotte (1997). Perceptual differences among visitor groups to wineries. *Journal of Travel Research, 35*(3): 46-51.

Getz, D. (2000). *Explore Wine Tourism: Management, Development and Destinations.* New York: Cognizant Communications Corporation.

Hall, C. M., Longo, A. M., Mitchell, R. D. & Johnson, G. R. (2000). Wine tourism in New Zealand. In C. M. Hall, E. Sharples, B. Cambourne, N. Macionis (eds.) *Wine Tourism Around the World.* Oxford: Butterworth Heinemann, 150-174.

Hinch, T. D. & Jackson, E. L. (2000). Leisure constraints research: Its value as a framework for understanding tourism seasonality. *Current Issues in Tourism, 3*(2), 87-106.

Jackson, E. (2000). *Tourism Tasmania: Wine Survey 2000.* Unpublished report. Hobart: Tourism Tasmania.

Johnson, G. R. (1998). *Wine Tourism in New Zealand: A National Survey of Wineries 1997.* Unpublished Dip. Tour. Dissertation, University of Otago.

Keown, C. and Casey, M. (1994). Purchasing behaviour in the Northern Ireland wine market. *British Food Journal, 97*(1): 17-20.

King, J. (2000). *Recognising and Defining Wine Tourism.* Unpublished report, Global Tourism & Leisure.

Koerber, K. (2000). Fueling increased. *Wine Business Monthly, 7*(5) [online edition].

Longo, A. M. (1999). *Wine Tourism in New Zealand: An exploration of the characteristics and motivations of winery visitors.* Unpublished Dip. Tour. Dissertation, University of Otago.

Machin, R. (2000). *'Quaffing through the Bay': An examination of wine tourism in Hawke's Bay.* Unpublished Dip. Tour. Dissertation, University of Otago.

Maddern, C. & Golledge, S. (1996). *Victorian Wineries Tourism Council Cellar Door Survey, Final Report May 1996.* Melbourne: Victorian Wineries Tourism Council.

Mitchell, R. & Hall, C. M. (2001a). The influence of gender and region on the New Zealand winery visit. *Tourism Recreation Research, 26*(2), 63-75.

Mitchell, R. & Hall, C. M. (2001b). Wine at home: Self-ascribed wine knowledge and the wine behavior of New Zealand winery visitors. *Australian and New Zealand Wine Industry Journal, 16*(6), 115-122.

Morris, R. & King, C. (1997). *The Cellar Door Report: Margaret River Region Winery Tourism Research.* Perth: Edith Cowan University.

Murphy, H. L. (1999). Xer's vintage point. *Marketing News, 33*(5) [online edition].

New Zealand Winegrowers (2002). Wine Institute Membership http://www.nzwine. com/statistics/ [accessed: 17/07/2002].

O'Neill, M. & Charters, S. (1999). Service quality at the cellar door: Implications for Western Australia's developing wine industry. *Managing Service Quality, 10*(2), 112-122.

O'Neill, M. & Charters, S. (2000). Delighting the customer–how good is the cellar door experience? *International Wine Marketing Supplement, 1*(1), 11-16.

Sansoni, S. (1998). Hey dude, slam that Beaujolais! *Forbes, 162*(1) [online edition].

Scarpa, J. (1999). X-appeal. *Restaurant Business, 98*(23) [online edition].

Stanford, L. (2000). What Australians drink, and when and where. *Australian and New Zealand Wine Industry Journal*, *15*(1), 14-27.

Statistics New Zealand (2002). *Accommodation Pivot Tables* http://www.stats.govt. nz/domino/external/web/prod_serv.nsf/3153e23ac69cb3d84c25680800821fa4/ d2625160cdd32850cc256b120074d2c0?OpenDocument [accessed: 17 April 2002].

The Wine Club (2000). *The Wine Club's '2000 Survey' Spotlights Buying Habits of California's Top Wine Consumers* http://www.just-drinks.com [accessed: 14 January 2001].

Index

SPECIAL 25%-OFF DISCOUNT!

Order a copy of this book with this form or online at:
http://www.haworthpress.com/store/product.asp?sku=5036
Use Sale Code BOF25 in the online bookshop to receive 25% off!

Wine, Food, and Tourism Marketing

___ in softbound at $18.71 (regularly $24.95) (ISBN: 0-7890-0106-3)
___ in hardbound at $29.96 (regularly $39.95) (ISBN: 0-7890-0082-2)

COST OF BOOKS _____	❏ **BILL ME LATER:** ($5 service charge will be added)
Outside USA/ Canada/	(Bill-me option is good on US/Canada/
Mexico: Add 20% _____	Mexico orders only; not good to jobbers,
POSTAGE & HANDLING _____	wholesalers, or subscription agencies.)
(US: $4.00 for first book & $1.50	❏ **Signature** _____
for each additional book)	
Outside US: $5.00 for first book	❏ **Payment Enclosed: $** _____
& $2.00 for each additional book)	❏ **PLEASE CHARGE TO MY CREDIT CARD:**
SUBTOTAL _____	❏ Visa ❏ MasterCard ❏ AmEx ❏ Discover
in Canada: add 7% GST _____	❏ Diner's Club ❏ Eurocard ❏ JCB
STATE TAX _____	**Account #**_____
(CA, IN, MIN, NY, OH, & SD residents	
please add appropriate local sales tax	**Exp Date** _____
FINAL TOTAL _____	**Signature**_____
(if paying in Canadian funds, convert	*(Prices in US dollars and subject to*
using the current exchange rate,	*change without notice.)*
UNESCO coupons welcome)	

PLEASE PRINT ALL INFORMATION OR ATTACH YOUR BUSINESS CARD

Name
Address
City   State/Province   Zip/Postal Code
Country
Tel   Fax
E-Mail

May we use your e-mail address for confirmations and other types of information? ❏Yes❏ No
We appreciate receiving your e-mail address. Haworth would like to e-mail special discount
offers to you, as a preferred customer. **We will never share, rent, or exchange your e-mail
address.** We regard such actions as an invasion of your privacy.

Order From Your Local Bookstore or Directly From
The Haworth Press, Inc.
10 Alice Street, Binghamton, New York 13904-1580 • USA
Call Our toll-free number (1-800-429-6784) / Outside US/Canada: (607) 722-5857
Fax: 1-800-895-0582 / Outside US/Canada: (607) 771-0012
E-Mail your order to us: Orders@haworthpress.com

Please Photocopy this form for your personal use.
www.HaworthPress.com

BOF03